1 Peter

EDITING AND PRODUCTION TEAM:

James F. Couch, Jr., Lyman Coleman, Sharon Penington, Cathy Tardif, Christopher Werner, Matthew Lockhart, Richard Peace, Erika Tiepel, Andrew Sloan, Gregory C. Benoit, Katharine Harris, Scott Lee

Staying the Course - 1 Peter
© 2003, 1998, 1988 Serendipity House
Reprinted May 2008

Published by Serendipity House Publishers
Nashville, Tennessee

ISBN: 1-5749-4329-4
Item 001197659

To purchase additional copies of this resource or other studies:
ORDER ONLINE at www.SerendipityHouse.com
WRITE Serendipity House, One LifeWay Plaza, Nashville, TN 37234-0175
FAX 615-277-8181
PHONE 800-458-2772

SERENDIPITY®
H O U S E
1-800-458-2772
www.SerendipityHouse.com

Printed in the United States of America

Table of Contents

Core Values

Community: The purpose of this curriculum is to build community within the body of believers around Jesus Christ.

Group Process: To build community, the curriculum must be designed to take a group through a step-by-step process of sharing your story with one another.

Interactive Bible Study: To share your "story," the approach to Scripture in the curriculum needs to be open-ended and right brain—to "level the playing field" and encourage everyone to share.

Developmental Stages: To provide a healthy program throughout the four stages of the life cycle of a group, the curriculum needs to offer courses on three levels of commitment: (1) Beginner Level—low-level entry, high structure, to level the playing field; (2) Growth Level—deeper Bible study, flexible structure, to encourage group accountability; (3) Discipleship Level—in-depth Bible study, open structure, to move the group into high gear.

Target Audiences: To build community throughout the culture of the church, the curriculum needs to be flexible, adaptable and transferable into the structure of the average church.

Mission: To expand the Kingdom of God one person at a time by filling the "empty chair." (We add an extra chair to each group session to remind us of our mission.)

Introduction

Each healthy small group will move through various stages as it matures.

Multiply Stage: The group begins the multiplication process. Members pray about their involvement in new groups. The "new" groups begin the life cycle again with the Birth Stage.

Birth Stage: This is the time in which group members form relationships and begin to develop community. The group will spend more time in ice-breaker exercises, relational Bible study and covenant building.

Develop Stage: The inductive Bible study deepens while the group members discover and develop gifts and skills. The group explores ways to invite their neighbors and coworkers to group meetings.

Growth Stage: Here the group begins to care for one another as it learns to apply what they learn through Bible study, worship and prayer.

 Subgrouping: If you have nine or more people at a meeting, Serendipity recommends you divide into subgroups of 3–6 for the Bible study. Ask one person to be the leader of each subgroup and to follow the directions for the Bible study. After 30 minutes, the Group Leader will call "time" and ask all subgroups to come together for the Caring Time.

Each group meeting should include all parts of the "three-part agenda."

 Ice-Breaker: Fun, history-giving questions are designed to warm the group and to build understanding about the other group members. You can choose to use all of the Ice-Breaker questions, especially if there is a new group member that will need help in feeling comfortable with the group.

 Bible Study: The heart of each meeting is the reading and examination of the Bible. The questions are open, discover questions that lead to further inquiry. Reference notes are provided to give everyone a "level playing field." The emphasis is on understanding what the Bible says and applying the truth to real life. The questions for each session build. There is always at least one "going deeper" question provided. You should always leave time for the last of the "questions for interaction." Should you choose, you can use the optional "going deeper" question to satisfy the desire for the challenging questions in groups that have been together for a while.

 Caring Time: All study should point us to actions. Each session ends with prayer and direction in caring for the needs of the group members. You can choose between several questions. You should always pray for the "empty chair." Who do you know that could fill that void in your group?

Sharing Your Story: These sessions are designed for members to share a little of their personal lives each time. Through a number of special techniques, each member is encouraged to move from low risk, less personal sharing to higher risk responses. This helps develop the sense of community and facilitates caregiving.

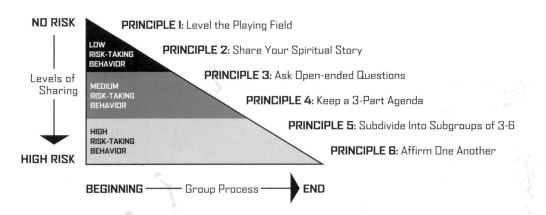

1 Peter

Staying the Course

SERENDIPITY
by LifeWay.

Group Directory

Pass this Directory around and have your Group Members
fill in their names and phone numbers

Name   **Phone**

_____   _____

_____   _____

_____   _____

_____   _____

_____   _____

_____   _____

_____   _____

_____   _____

_____   _____

_____   _____

_____   _____

_____   _____

_____   _____

_____   _____

_____   _____

Group Covenant: A group covenant is a "contract" that spells out your expectations and the ground rules for your group. It's very important that your group discuss these issues—preferably as part of the first session.

Ground Rules:

• Priority: While you are in the group, you give the group meeting priority.

• Participation: Everyone participates and no one dominates.

• Respect: Everyone is given the right to their own opinion and all questions are encouraged and respected.

• Confidentiality: Anything that is said in the meeting is never repeated outside the meeting.

• Empty Chair: The group stays open to new people at every meeting.

• Support: Permission is given to call upon each other in time of need—even in the middle of the night.

• Advice Giving: Unsolicited advice is not allowed.

• Mission: We agree to do everything in our power to start a new group as our mission.

Goals:

• The time and place this group is going to meet is_____.

• Responsibility for refreshments is _____.

• Child care is _____ responsibility.

• This group will meet until _____ at which time we will decide to split into new groups or continue our sessions together.

• Our primary purpose for meeting is _____

Ten Steps for Multiplying Small Groups

1. **Share a vision:** From the very first meeting of a group the vision must be cast for the mission. God can greatly affect the larger body of Christ through a small group if there is a vision for creating new groups and bringing people into the kingdom. If the group will make a group covenant that envisions multiplying into new groups, then new groups will happen. An effective leader will regularly keep this goal in front of the group. It is essential to raise up group leaders from your group and to divide into new groups every 18–24 months. Announce the intention to multiply early and often.

2. **Build a new leadership team:** As the group matures through the Growth and Develop Stages, the present leadership team should identify apprentice leaders and facilitators. This is done best in a small group setting. Look for an engineer type as the group administrator, the party animal as the hospitality person, a person that loves interaction and knowledge as the facilitator and a caring person to handle group shepherding. Next you must seek to train and mentor them as they grow in confidence. Here is an outline of this process:

    a. Identify apprentice leaders and facilitators
    b. Provide on-the-job training
    c. Give them the opportunity to lead your group
    d. Introduce the new team to your church
    e. Launch the new group

3. **Determine the type of group:** Who are you trying to reach? Here are four commonly identified audiences.

Group		Percentage	Group Type
a.	Core	10%	Discipleship Group
b.	Congregation	30%	Pulpit or Care Groups
c.	Crowd	60%	Felt Need Groups
d.	Seekers	Outsiders	Support Groups
e.		All	Affinity Groups
f.		All	Covenant Groups

4. **Conduct a Felt Need Survey:** Use either a custom survey for your church or the one included in this book to determine an area or a specific topic for your first study.

5. **Choose curriculum:** Make sure your choice fits the group type and the stage in the life cycle of your group. All Serendipity courses are pre-selected for stage of the life cycle.

6. **Ask someone to serve as host:** Determine when and where the group will meet. Someone must coordinate the following.

    a. Where the meeting will be held.
    b. Who will provide babysitters (if necessary).
    c. Who will teach children (if necessary).
    d. Who will provide refreshments.

7. **Find out who will go with the new team:** There are several options in beginning new groups.

    a. Encourage several members of your group to go with the new leadership team to start a new group.

    b. The existing leadership team will leave to start a new group leaving the existing group with the new team.

    c. Several groups can break off beginning all new groups.

8. **Begin countdown:** Use a study designed to help multiply groups, building each week until you launch your new group.

9. **Celebrate:** Have a party with presents for the new group. Make announcements to your church, advertising the new group and its leadership team.

10. **Keep casting a vision:** Remember as you start new groups to keep casting a vision for multiplying into new groups.

Leadership Team for Small Groups

Coordinator: Is responsible to the church leadership team for:
1. Building a leadership team.
2. Ensuring the coordination of the group.
3. Meeting with the leadership team once a month for encouragement and planning.
4. Casting a vision for multiplication and beginning the process of multiplication.

Facilitating Team: Is responsible to the coordinator for:
1. Guiding the group in life-changing Bible study.
2. Developing a facilitating team for subgrouping into groups of three to six.
3. Keeping the group on agenda, but being sensitive when someone needs to share.
4. Subdividing the group for Bible study and caring time and emphasizing the "empty chair."

Care Team: Is responsible to the coordinator for:
1. Contacting group members to encourage attendance and personal growth.
2. Keeping the group informed of prayer needs.
3. Coordinating caring for the special needs of the group.

Party Team: Is responsible to the coordinator for:
1. Planning, coordinating and promoting monthly group parties.
2. Keeping the members involved in the party activities.

Host/Hostess: Is responsible to the coordinator for:
1. Providing a clean home with enough space to subdivide into groups of three to six.
2. Coordinating refreshments.
3. Welcoming guests and having name tags at each meeting.
4. Making sure everything is conducive for sharing (no TV, comfortable temperature, arrangements for children).

Felt Need Survey

Rank the following factor in order of importance to you with 1 being the highest and five being the lowest:

_____ The passage of Scripture that is being studied.

_____ The topic or issue that is being discussed.

_____ The affinity of group members (age, vocation, interest).

_____ The mission of the group (service projects, evangelism, starting groups).

_____ Personal encouragement.

Rank the following spiritual development needs in order of interest to you with 1 being the highest and 5 being the lowest:

_____ Learning how to become a follower of Christ.

_____ Gaining a basic understanding of the truths of the faith.

_____ Improving my disciplines of devotion, prayer, reading Scripture.

_____ Gaining a better knowledge of what is in the Bible.

_____ Applying the truths of Scripture to my life.

Of the various studies below check the appropriate boxes that indicate: if you would be interested in studying for your personal needs (P), you think would be helpful for your group (G), or you have friends that are not in the groups that would come to a group studying this subject (F).

	P	G	F
Growing in Christ Series (7-week studies)			
Keeping Your Cool: Dealing With Stress	☐	☐	☐
Personal Audit: Assessing Your Life	☐	☐	☐
Seasons of Growth: Stages of Marriage	☐	☐	☐
Checking Your Moral Compass: Personal Morals	☐	☐	☐
Women of Faith (8 weeks)	☐	☐	☐
Men of Faith	☐	☐	☐
Being Single and the Spiritual Quest	☐	☐	☐
Becoming a Disciple (7-week studies)			
Discovering God's Will	☐	☐	☐
Time for a Checkup	☐	☐	☐
Learning to Love	☐	☐	☐
Making Great Kids	☐	☐	☐
Becoming Small Group Leaders	☐	☐	☐
Foundations of the Faith (7-week studies)			
Knowing Jesus	☐	☐	☐
Foundational Truths	☐	☐	☐
The Christian in a Postmodern World	☐	☐	☐
God and the Journey to Truth	☐	☐	☐

	P	G	F
Understanding the Savior (13-week studies)			
Mark 1–8: Jesus, the Early Years	❑	❑	❑
Mark 8–16: Jesus, the Final Days	❑	❑	❑
John 1–11: God in the Flesh	❑	❑	❑
John 12–21: The Passion of the Son	❑	❑	❑
The Miracles of Jesus	❑	❑	❑
The Life of Christ	❑	❑	❑
The Parables of Jesus	❑	❑	❑
The Sermon on the Mount: Jesus, the Teacher	❑	❑	❑
The Message of Paul			
Romans 1–7: Who We Really Are (13 weeks)	❑	❑	❑
Romans 8–16: Being a Part of God's Plan (13 weeks)	❑	❑	❑
1 Corinthians: Taking on Tough Issues (13 weeks)	❑	❑	❑
Galatians: Living by Grace (13 weeks)	❑	❑	❑
Ephesians: Together in Christ (12 weeks)	❑	❑	❑
Philippians: Running the Race (7 weeks)	❑	❑	❑
Words of Faith			
Acts 1–14: The Church on Fire (13 weeks)	❑	❑	❑
Acts 15–28: The Irrepressible Witness (13 weeks)	❑	❑	❑
Hebrews: The True Messiah (13 weeks)	❑	❑	❑
James: Faith at Work (12 weeks)	❑	❑	❑
1 Peter: Staying the Course (10 weeks)	❑	❑	❑
1 John: Walking in the Light (11 weeks)	❑	❑	❑
Revelation 1–12: End of Time (13 weeks)	❑	❑	❑
Revelation 13–22: The New Jerusalem (13 weeks)	❑	❑	❑
301 Bible Studies with Homework Assignments (13-week studies)			
Ephesians: Our Riches in Christ	❑	❑	❑
James: Walking the Talk	❑	❑	❑
Life of Christ: Behold the Man	❑	❑	❑
Miracles: Signs and Wonders	❑	❑	❑
Parables: Virtual Reality	❑	❑	❑
Philippians: Joy Under Stress	❑	❑	❑
Sermon on the Mount: Examining Your Life	❑	❑	❑
1 John: The Test of Faith	❑	❑	❑
Felt Need Series (7-week studies)			
Stress Management: Finding the Balance	❑	❑	❑
12 Steps: The Path to Wholeness	❑	❑	❑
Divorce Recovery: Picking Up the Pieces	❑	❑	❑
Parenting Adolescents: Easing the Way to Adulthood	❑	❑	❑
Blended Families: Yours, Mine, Ours	❑	❑	❑
Dealing with Grief and Loss: Hope in the Midst of Pain	❑	❑	❑
Healthy Relationships: Living Within Defined Boundaries	❑	❑	❑
Marriage Enrichment: Making a Good Marriage Better	❑	❑	❑

Other great resources from Serendipity House...

MORE

More depth, more meaning, more life.

Discovering truth through Bible study is much more than breaking a verse down to its smallest part and deconstructing a passage word by word. There is context and experience, mystery and story that all go into fully understanding the Word of God. By dissecting down to the smallest part, we often lose the essence of the whole. For this reason, Serendipity introduces a new approach to the inductive Bible-study format that looks at each passage within the context of the larger story. This reunifies the cognitive aspect with an experiential dynamic and allows the truths of scripture to come alive in new and unexpected ways.

Song of Songs: The Epic Romance | 1574943405
Job: A Messy Faith | 1574943464

Mark: Beyond the Red Letters | 1574943413
Colossians: Embrace the Mystery | 1574944150

GOD AND THE ARTS

Where faith intersects life.

Stories, great and small, share the same essential structure because every story we tell borrows its power from a Larger Story. What we sense stirring within is a heart that is made for a place in the Larger Story. It is no accident that great movies include a hero, a villain, a betrayal, a battle to fight, a romance, and a beauty to rescue. It is The Epic story and it is truer than anything we know. Adventure awaits. Listen.

Discover an experience that guides you on a journey into the one great Epic in which the Bible is set. These fun and provocative studies features four films, each with two small-group meetings, *Dinner and a Movie* (Week 1), *Connecting the Dots* (Week 2), and an *Experience Guide* that offers valuable insights.

Finding Jesus in the Movies | 1574943553
Finding Redemption in the Movies | 1574943421

Greetings

SCRIPTURE 1 PETER 1:1-2

 ## Welcome

Welcome to this study of 1 Peter. This book is actually a "circular letter," written to Christians living in the northwest section of Asia Minor (what is now modern Turkey). This was a huge area with a large population. The letter itself would have been carried from church to church, read aloud to the believers at each stop.

The Christians to whom Peter writes were mainly Gentiles, as is clear from the way in which he describes their pre-conversion lifestyle. Peter uses categories and phrases that typically were applied to pagans, not Jews (1:14; 2:9–10; 4:3–4).

Peter wrote this letter to bring hope and strength to men and women who were being persecuted because they were Christians. At the time he wrote, such harassment was new. For the first three decades of its existence, the church was protected, not persecuted, by the Roman Empire.

All this changed on July 19, A.D. 64. That night, Rome caught fire. For three days and nights the fire blazed out of control. Ancient temples and historic landmarks were swept away by the ferocity of the blaze. Homes were destroyed. The citizens of Rome were distraught and they were angry. It was widely felt that Nero, the emperor, was the one responsible for the fire. Nero tried to squelch these rumors, but they persisted nonetheless. In desperation, he created a scapegoat: he blamed the fire on the Christians. In so doing, Nero introduced the church to martyrdom. The persecution that began in Rome would soon spread across the empire.

Christians were now technically outlaws and thus subject to persecution. They were torn to pieces by dogs, crucified, even made into torches to be ignited after dark in Nero's gardens. Peter writes to those Christians in Asia Minor who were going through such persecution. He says to them, "As you share in the sufferings of the Messiah, rejoice" (4:13). At first glance, this seems to be a strange thing to say. How can they rejoice when times are so tough? The answer Peter gives is that rejoicing is possible because of the great hope they have as Christians. Hope is the theme of Peter's letter to these suffering Christians.

As with other ancient letters, it is not possible to give a precise date for the composition of 1 Peter. However, if this letter was sparked by Nero's persecution, and if Peter died in Rome in A.D. 68, as tradition has it, then it must have been written in the mid-60s.

Ice-Breaker

CONNECT WITH YOUR GROUP

LEADER

Be sure to read the introductory material in the front of this book prior to this first session. To help your group members get acquainted, have each person introduce him or herself and then take turns answering one or two of the Ice-Breaker questions. If time allows, you may want to discuss all three questions.

As we begin our study of 1 Peter, we will discover immediately that the circumstances of our lives cannot last forever. This is because we, as Christians, do not belong to this world but to the kingdom of God. Take some time to get to know one another better by sharing your responses to the following questions.

1. Who is the person that you correspond with most often?

- ○ Parent.
- ○ Other family member.
- ○ Close friend.
- ○ Person you are dating.
- ○ Someone who owes you money.
- ○ Other _____.

2 How many times did your family move when you were growing up? Which time was the hardest?

3. How geographically scattered is your family now? How often do you get together?

Bible Study

READ SCRIPTURE AND DISCUSS

LEADER

Select a member of the group ahead of time to read aloud the Scripture passage. Then discuss the Questions for Interaction, dividing into subgroups of three to six. Be sure to save time at the end for the Caring Time.

Peter introduces his letter by addressing his audience as "temporary residents" who have been "chosen" by God. This tells his listeners right up front that they are not really citizens of this world, regardless of what they might be experiencing, but their true citizenship is in heaven. Read 1 Peter 1:1–2, and note how this is true, not because of their own lives or experiences, but because God has chosen them.

Greetings

1 Peter, an apostle of Jesus Christ:
To the temporary residents of the Dispersion in the provinces of Pontus, Galatia, Cappadocia, Asia, and Bithynia, chosen ²according to the foreknowledge of God the Father and set apart by the Spirit for obedience and for the sprinkling with the blood of Jesus Christ.
May grace and peace be multiplied to you.

1 Peter 1:1–2

QUESTIONS FOR INTERACTION

Refer to the Summary and Study Notes at the end of this session as needed. If 30 minutes is not enough time to answer all of the questions in this section, conclude the Bible Study by answering question 7.

1. When have you most felt like a stranger?

○ After a move.
○ When changing schools.
○ In a new job.
○ At a new church.
○ Other _____.

2. Why does Peter refer to these Christians as "temporary residents" of Asia Minor?

3. If these believers are "temporary residents," what does that imply about their sufferings? Their potential martyrdom?

4. Why does Peter say that these people were "chosen according to the foreknowledge of God the Father"? How might God's foreknowledge give them hope in the face of persecution?

5. Peter says that Christians are "set apart ... for obedience." What does this mean to us today? What power do believers have to help with obedience?

6. If you are a temporary resident of this planet, how should that affect your view of your own life?

7. How can you find encouragement in the fact that God has "foreknowledge" of all that you will face in life?

GOING DEEPER:

If your group has time and/or wants a challenge, go on to this question.

8. Peter also says that Christians are set apart "for the sprinkling with the blood of Jesus Christ." What does this mean? Does it imply a sense of cleansing through suffering?

Caring Time   15 Min.

APPLY THE LESSON AND PRAY FOR ONE ANOTHER

This very important time is for developing and expressing your concern for each other as group members by praying for one another.

Take some extra time in this first session to go over the introductory material at the beginning of this book. At the close, pass around your books and have everyone sign the Group Directory in the front of the book.

1. Agree on the group covenant and ground rules that are described in the introduction to this book.

2. With what area of obedience in your life have you recently been struggling?

3. Share any other prayer requests and praises, and then close in prayer. Pray specifically for God to lead you to someone to bring next week to fill the empty chair.

Next Week

Today we considered how we are just living on earth temporarily, and that whatever pleasures or heartaches or persecution we may be experiencing now will not last indefinitely. In the coming week, examine your own life and attitudes and strive to remember that everything in this world, good and bad, will pass away. Next week we will learn about the "living hope" that is part of our eternal inheritance, something that will not pass away.

Notes on 1 Peter 1:1—2

SUMMARY: Peter begins his letter in the way most Greek letters began in the first century. He first identifies himself as the writer and then identifies those to whom his letter is written. He concludes the salutation with his own version of the standard Christian greeting: "May grace and peace be multiplied to you."

In the process of identifying those to whom he is writing, Peter gives us rich insight into what it means to be a Christian. In relationship to God, Christians are "elect." They are chosen by the Father; this choice is activated by the Holy Spirit and it is made possible by the Son. (This is an early formulation of the doctrine of the Trinity.) In relationship to the world, Christians are "strangers," "scattered" throughout the world.

1:1 *Peter.* Peter was the leader of the 12 apostles. Before joining Jesus' band of disciples he was a fisherman on the Sea of Galilee. He worked with his brother Andrew in partnership with James and John (Luke 5:10). Their business was based in Capernaum where Peter and Andrew lived together (Mark 1:21,29). Peter was married (Mark 1:30). Later in his ministry he took his wife with him on visits to the churches (1 Cor. 9:5). His father's name was Jonah (Matt. 16:17). Peter, along with his brother Andrew, was one of the first chosen to be a disciple of Jesus (Mark 1:16–18).

Peter was the most prominent of the disciples. In every list of the Twelve, he is mentioned first. The reason for this is clear. Peter often took the initiative in situations (as when he volunteered to walk to Jesus across the water—Matt. 14:28). He generally spoke for the disciples (as at Caesarea Philippi when he answered Jesus' question about who he was—Mark 8:29). Peter was also part of the inner circle of disciples (Peter, James and John) with whom Jesus had the most intimate relationship. He was the first of the Twelve to see the resurrected Jesus (1 Cor. 15:5). During the early years after the Resurrection, Peter was the dominant force in the church. He was a powerful preacher through whom thousands came to faith (Acts 2:14–41); he worked miracles, including raising a woman from the dead (Acts 9:36–42); he spearheaded outreach to Jews living outside Jerusalem (Acts 8:14; 9:32–35); and he was responsible for allowing Gentiles to be baptized without first converting to Judaism (Acts 10:1–11:18). The first 12 chapters of Acts focus on his role in the early church. Tradition has it that Peter was crucified upside-down in Rome in the mid to late A.D. 60s.

Peter is known by four names in the New Testament: Simeon, his Hebrew name (Acts 15:14); Simon, a Greek name (Mark 1:16); Peter, the name that Jesus gave to him (John 1:42) and which he uses here; and Cephas, which is the Aramaic version of Peter. Peter is his "Christian" name and means "a stone" or "a rock." *an apostle.* This means, literally, "one who is sent." It is the term used in the New Testament to identify those who were selected for the special task of founding and guiding the new church. To be an apostle one had to be a witness to the resurrection of Jesus. *temporary residents.* The Greek word used here is *parepidemoi.* It means "sojourner" and refers to those who are far from home, dwelling in a strange land. The term is used metaphorically for Christians, whose true home is in heaven. *Dispersion.* The Greek word here is *diaspora,* which means "the dispersion." It originally referred to those Jews who were scattered in exile throughout a number of countries outside Palestine. Once again, Peter uses a term originally applied to Israel to refer to the church. *Pontus, Galatia, Cappadocia, Asia, and Bithynia.* These are Roman provinces located in Asia Minor (now modern Turkey). The order in which they are named is the order in which a traveler would visit each.

1:2 Peter has already referred to the Christians as "God's elect." In this verse he points out the role of God the Father, God the Son and God the Holy Spirit in the process of election. The doctrine of the Trinity emerged out of the experience of the people. *chosen according to the foreknowledge of God the Father.* Israel knew itself to be chosen (selected, elected, picked) by God to be his people (Ezek. 20:5; Hos. 11:1). They were to be the people through whom he would reveal himself to the rest of the world. The first Christians knew that they too had been chosen by God. *foreknowledge.* It is not just a matter of God knowing something before it happens. What God foreknows he brings to pass. Here his purpose is defined as "obedience to Jesus." *set apart by the Spirit.* The choice of God takes effect by the work of the Holy Spirit. The aim of the work of the Spirit is holiness. The Holy Spirit awakens in people the longing for God, convicts them of their sin, and opens them to the saving power of Jesus' death. Following conversion, the Spirit continues this sanctifying work by bringing power to overcome sin, assurance of sins forgiven, and new ways of living and feeling (the fruit of the Spirit). *for obedience.* The aim of this chosenness is obedience to Christ. The obedience referred to here is not the daily obedience of the believer. *sprinkling with the blood.* It is by means of the death of Christ that election is made possible. His death opened the way back to God. The image of sprinkling with blood comes from the Jewish sacrificial system. The primary Old Testament reference is to the acceptance of the covenant by the people of Israel (Ex. 24:1–8). God expressed his choice of Israel by means of a covenant in which he agreed to be their God and they agreed to obey him. Moses took half the blood of the sacrificial animals and sprinkled it on the altar and the other half on the people, thus sealing their commitment. *grace and peace.* At this point in a letter, the typical Greek writer would usually say simply: "Greetings." However, Peter and other New Testament writers (e.g. Paul, see Phil. 1:2) Christianized this statement by adding the Hebrew greeting "shalom," meaning "peace."

SESSION 2
A Living Hope
SCRIPTURE 1 PETER 1:3-12

 ## Last Week

In our previous session, we discovered that followers of Jesus Christ are not citizens of this world, but rather have their true home in the kingdom of God. This week we will learn about one of the real treasures that we do possess, a "living hope," which God is keeping secure in heaven.

Ice-Breaker   15 Min.

CONNECT WITH YOUR GROUP

Begin the session with a word of prayer. Have your group members take turns sharing their responses to one, two or all three of the Ice-Breaker questions. Be sure that everyone gets a chance to participate.

In our passage this week, Peter will describe for us one of the great joys of our salvation—a glorious hope in eternity that can never be taken away from us. This is so exciting and so grand a mystery that "angels desire to look into" it but cannot fathom it. Take turns sharing your thoughts and experiences with good news and thankfulness.

1. As a child, did you own something that seemed priceless to you? Is it still priceless today?

2. What do you like to do to celebrate good news?

    ◯ Throw a party.
    ◯ Call everyone I know.
    ◯ Write in a journal.
    ◯ Pray.
    ◯ Other _____.

3. What is something for which you are particularly thankful?

READ SCRIPTURE AND DISCUSS

LEADER

Select a group member ahead of time to read aloud the Scripture passage. Then discuss the Questions for Interaction, dividing into subgroups of three to six.

In this section, Peter addresses the sufferings of his audience, but also turns their focus away from their present affliction toward an eternal hope, a "living hope" that can never fade or be taken away. Read 1 Peter 1:3–12, and note how he also gives the suffering believers insight into some of the reasons for their sufferings.

A Living Hope

³Blessed be the God and Father of our Lord Jesus Christ. According to His great mercy, He has given us a new birth into a living hope through the resurrection of Jesus Christ from the dead, ⁴and into an inheritance that is imperishable, uncorrupted, and unfading, kept in heaven for you, ⁵who are being protected by God's power through faith for a salvation that is ready to be revealed in the last time. ⁶You rejoice in this, though now for a short time you have had to be distressed by various trials ⁷so that the genuineness of your faith—more valuable than gold, which perishes though refined by fire—may result in praise, glory, and honor at the revelation of Jesus Christ. ⁸You love Him, though you have not seen Him. And though not seeing Him now, you believe in Him and rejoice with inexpressible and glorious joy, ⁹because you are receiving the goal of your faith, the salvation of your souls.

¹⁰Concerning this salvation, the prophets who prophesied about the grace that would come to you searched and carefully investigated. ¹¹They inquired into what time or what circumstances the Spirit of Christ within them was indicating when He testified in advance to the messianic sufferings and the glories that would follow. ¹²It was revealed to them that they were not serving themselves but you concerning things that have now been announced to you through those who preached the gospel to you by the Holy Spirit sent from heaven. Angels desire to look into these things.

1 Peter 1:3–12

QUESTIONS FOR INTERACTION

LEADER

Refer to the Summary and Study Notes at the end of this session as needed. If 30 minutes is not enough time to answer all of the questions in this section, conclude the Bible Study by answering question 7.

1. When you were growing up, what was the worst trial your family ever faced?

2. Our hope is "imperishable, uncorrupted, and unfading" (v. 4). How does this compare with our earthly hopes, such as success, health or security?

3. Peter says that the believers in Asia Minor were "distressed by various trials" for a "short time" (v. 6). How do you think they felt as they were facing persecution and death? Why does Peter treat their sufferings this way?

4. What is the real purpose of sufferings, according to Peter?

5. Peter refers to the "messianic sufferings" of Christ and the "glories" that his death and resurrection produced (v. 11). How does this relate to the sufferings of the Christians under Nero? How does it relate to your own sufferings?

6. When has your faith been tested by a fiery trial? How did you come out of it? What are you going through right now that is helping to strengthen your faith?

7. Which point from this passage do you need the most right now?

❍ New birth.
❍ Hope for the future.
❍ Faith in God's power.
❍ Joy regardless of circumstances.
❍ Love for the Jesus that you've never seen.
❍ Other _____.

GOING DEEPER:

If your group has time and/or wants a challenge, go on to this question.

8. How did the prophets of Old Testament times actually serve us instead of themselves? How might our own lives be spent in serving future generations?

Caring Time _____ 15 Min.

APPLY THE LESSON AND PRAY FOR ONE ANOTHER

LEADER

Bring the group back together and begin the Caring Time by sharing responses to all three questions. Then take turns sharing prayer requests and having a time of group prayer. Be sure to include prayer for the empty chair.

Focus this week on serving one another, helping each other to undergo and endure trials. In this way, we can be like the prophets of old, who served us instead of themselves. Gather around each other now and support one another in a time of sharing and prayer.

1. Where did you place your treasure this past week? How will you consciously store it in heaven this coming week?

2. How can the group support you in your present trials?

3. Do you know someone outside this group who needs to be "served" by us?

P.S. *Add new group members to the Group Directory at the front of this book.*

Next Week

Today we considered how Christians have a hope that transcends everything we experience in this life, a hope more precious than the most valuable things of this world. In the coming week, spend time in prayer for others who may be undergoing trials or suffering. If there are other things you can do to help a suffering friend, do so. Next week we will learn about holiness and how a believer attains it.

Notes on 1 Peter 1:3–12

SUMMARY: Typically in a Greek letter, the salutation is followed by a word of thanksgiving to the gods for blessings received. Peter follows this pattern and in these verses praises God for the resurrection of Jesus Christ through which salvation came (vv. 3–5). The reality of this salvation brings rejoicing, which in turn upholds the church in the trials it must face until Jesus returns (vv. 6–9). He ends his prayer by recalling the long preparation for this salvation in the history of Israel (vv. 10–12).

Thus, Peter picks up on the themes found in his salutation and here spells out in more detail the identity of the people of God. The basis for their identity is the great salvation that God is bringing about. This salvation will be consummated in the future (vv. 3–5), though it is present in their daily experience (vv. 6–9) and it is rooted in the past (vv. 10–12).

1:3–5 Peter begins his letter with a powerful statement in which he focuses on the coming day of salvation. Two facts are singled out here for note. God has redeemed them and he has guarded them so that they will receive the full benefit of their salvation.

1:3 *Blessed be.* The phrase "praise be" or "blessed be" followed by the name of God was common in Jewish prayers (Ps. 68:19). It later was adopted by the Christian church (2 Cor. 1:3) and is used here by Peter. ***new birth.*** When people encounter Jesus, something so radical happens that they can be said to be reborn into a whole new life. This is no mere metaphor, but an accurate description of the transformation whereby a person becomes a part of the family of God and aware of spiritual reality. ***a living hope.*** This is the first thing new birth brings. Specifically here, their hope is that one day when Christ comes again they will experience the full fruit of salvation when they experience the resurrection life of Jesus. They have tasted this new life in the here and now, but they have not yet come into full possession of it. It is this hope that sustains them in hard times. ***the resurrection of Jesus Christ.***

That which makes salvation possible is the fact that Jesus rose from the dead and lives today as the powerful Lord of heaven and earth. His resurrection from death to life makes possible their rebirth to spiritual life.

1:4 *into an inheritance.* New birth also brings a secure inheritance. To be born again means they have become part of a new family, and like all sons and daughters they can expect an inheritance. ***imperishable, uncorrupted, and unfading.*** The first phrase, "imperishable," can also mean "unravaged by any invading army." The second phrase, "uncorrupted," refers to a land that has not been polluted or defiled by a conquering army. The third phrase, "unfading," paints a picture of a land without change or decay. It refers especially to flowers that do not fade. Taken together, these descriptions define a land that is radically different from the Promised Land that time and again was conquered, despoiled, and desecrated. ***kept in heaven for you.*** This inheritance is immune to disaster.

1:5 *protected.* Not only is the inheritance guarded and immune to disaster, but so too are the Christians for whom it exists. *salvation.* This is the object of the believers' hope and the content of their inheritance. The word "salvation" is used in several ways in the New Testament. The reference here is not to individual salvation, but to that moment in history when Christ will return again and all believers will come into the full enjoyment of eternity.

1:6 The experience of rebirth and the anticipation of an inheritance (both fruits of salvation) enable Christians to "greatly rejoice" despite trials and adversities. They know that these trials are only temporary (as stated here in v. 6), that they will get through them (v. 5), and that what lies ahead is the most real of all (v. 4). They can stand anything now because of what is theirs in the future. *for a short time you have had to be distressed.* By these two clauses, Peter gives perspective to their suffering. First, it will be temporary ("for a short time"). He may say this because he feels that the Lord's coming is near, or because in comparison with eternity what they are going through is but a moment. Second, such trials are circumstantial, perhaps even necessary ("you may have had to" or "if need be"). Trials simply come. Certain circumstances make them inevitable. However, such trials do not fall outside God's providence. *trials.* Peter's first allusion to their persecution. The language indicates that he has in mind actual difficulties they have faced and are facing.

1:7 Peter adds a third perspective. They can endure because these trials will have a positive benefit. They will reveal the quality of their faith. *genuineness.* This will make evident the actual quality and strength of the faith they possess. Such trials do not create faith; they reveal what is already there. *gold.* Gold was the most precious of metals in the first century. Their faith is worth even more! *fire.* Fire was used to burn away the impurities and so reveal the pure gold. In the same way, trials reveal the inner quality of faith. In an interesting twist, Peter notes that even though gold can stand up to fire, in the end it too, as part of the creation, will perish.

1:8 Most of the Christians to whom Peter writes would not have known Jesus when he was alive. But that doesn't matter. They still love him and have faith in him, with the result that they are filled with an overwhelming joy.

1:9 *you are receiving.* The verb means, literally, "carry off for oneself," and refers to a prize or a punishment one has earned. The tense of the verb indicates that this is a present reality. They are even now experiencing the salvation which they will fully realize only in the future.

1:10–12 The salvation that is still to come (vv. 3–5) and which is present even now (vv. 6–9) was in the past the object of longing on the part of prophets (vv. 10–12a) and even angels (v. 12b).

1:11 *inquired into.* In the era preceding Jesus, there was frantic seeking to know what God would do. Even the Old Testament prophets, as Peter points out here, had only a blurred vision of what was to come in God's grace. *the Spirit of Christ.* The pre-existent Christ was the one who inspired the prophets.

1:12 The Old Testament looked forward to the New Testament. There is a continuity and a unity between both parts of the Bible. What the prophets predicted was preached by the apostles. *It was revealed.* The process of revelation involves the searching and probing of prophets, coupled with and guided by the leading of the Spirit. In this way God reveals himself.

Be Holy

SCRIPTURE 1 PETER 1:13–2:3

Last Week

In last week's session, we learned that Christians have a living hope, an eternal salvation that is more valuable than the most costly gold. We also considered how the sufferings and pleasures of this life are only temporary and cannot compare to our long-term home in the kingdom of God. This week we will focus on how this hope requires that we live in a certain way, and on the fact that our pilgrimage on earth is to be lived out in holiness and love for one another.

Ice-Breaker   15 Min.

CONNECT WITH YOUR GROUP

Choose one or two Ice-Breaker questions. If you have a new group member you may want to do all three to help him or her get acquainted. Remember to stick closely to the three-part agenda and the time allowed for each segment.

Nobody is perfect, but all of us at times wish we were. Peter tells us today that we need to be a holy example to the rest of the world. Striving for perfection and holiness can be a real challenge. Take turns sharing some of your experiences with pursuing perfection.

1. How did you get ready for exams in school?

- ○ Studied regularly.
- ○ Crammed all night.
- ○ Got a good night's sleep.
- ○ Made up good "cheat sheets."
- ○ Other _____.

2. On a scale of 1 (totally disobedient) to 10 (perfect child), what kind of child were you?

3. Who do you know who is a "perfectionist?"

Have two group members, whom you have selected beforehand, read aloud the Scripture passage. Assign the Scripture as outlined. Then discuss the Questions for Interaction, dividing into subgroups of three to six.

In our passage this week, Peter moves on from his previous discussion of the eternal hope that we gain in Christ, to exhort us to live in holiness. He repeats the idea that we are "temporary residents" in this world, but this time with a new twist—if we are temporary residents, then we must not become attached to the things of this world. Read 1 Peter 1:13–2:3, and note how we are to achieve holiness.

Be Holy

Reader One: 13Therefore, get your minds ready for action, being self-disciplined, and set your hope completely on the grace to be brought to you at the revelation of Jesus Christ. 14As obedient children, do not be conformed to the desires of your former ignorance 15but, as the One who called you is holy, you also are to be holy in all your conduct; 16for it is written, "Be holy, because I am holy."

17And if you address as Father the One who judges impartially based on each one's work, you are to conduct yourselves in reverence during this time of temporary residence. 18For you know that you were redeemed from your empty way of life inherited from the fathers, not with perishable things, like silver or gold, 19but with the precious blood of Christ, like that of a lamb without defect or blemish. 20He was destined before the foundation of the world, but was revealed at the end of the times for you 21who through Him are believers in God, who raised Him from the dead and gave Him glory, so that your faith and hope are in God.

Reader Two: 22By obedience to the truth, having purified yourselves for sincere love of the brothers, love one another earnestly from a pure heart, 23since you have been born again—not of perishable seed but of imperishable—through the living and enduring word of God. 24For

> "All flesh is like grass,
> and all its glory like a flower of the grass.
> The grass withers, and the flower drops off,
> 25but the word of the Lord endures forever."

And this is the word that was preached as the gospel to you.

2 So rid yourselves of all wickedness, all deceit, hypocrisy, envy, and all slander. 2Like newborn infants, desire the unadulterated spiritual milk, so that you may grow by it in your salvation, 3since you have tasted that the Lord is good.

1 Peter 1:13–2:3

QUESTIONS FOR INTERACTION

Refer to the Summary and Study Notes at the end of this session as needed. If 30 minutes is not enough time to answer all of the questions in this section, conclude the Bible Study by answering question 7.

1. What sort of "action" (1:13) is your mind ready for?

○ Pleasure.
○ Success.
○ Anxiety.
○ Dinner.
○ Holiness.
○ Other _____.

2. Peter tells his audience to "set your hope completely on the grace to be brought to you" (1:13). How might this have helped the Christians in Asia Minor? How can it help us today?

3. Why does Peter remind us that we have been redeemed "with the precious blood of Christ" (1:19)? How is this an important concept in the struggle to live in holiness?

4. What kind of holiness does Peter call us to? How does this call challenge you at home, work, church, or in your neighborhood?

5. How does being "born again" help Christians "love one another earnestly from a pure heart" (1:22–23)?

6. How does following the command in 2:1 help us to practice loving one another from pure hearts? What grade would you give yourself on loving others lately?

7. How much do you struggle with being drawn back to the "desires of your former ignorance" (1:14) that you had before becoming a Christian? How can focusing on the precious blood of Christ help?

GOING DEEPER:

If your group has time and/or wants a challenge, go on to this question.

8. What is the "unadulterated spiritual milk" that we are to desire (2:2)? In what way do you still need this milk?

Caring Time

APPLY THE LESSON AND PRAY FOR ONE ANOTHER

LEADER

Begin the Caring Time by having group members take turns sharing responses to all three questions. Be sure to save at least the last five minutes for a time of group prayer. Remember to include a prayer for the empty chair when concluding the prayer time.

Encouraging and supporting each other is especially vital if this group is to become all it can be. Take time now to build up one another in love with sharing and prayer.

1. What is the best thing that happened to you last week? What is the worst?

2. Is your mind "ready for action" and "self-disciplined?" How can the group pray for you in this area?

3. How is the group doing in the area of loving one another? What can we do together to increase our mutual caring and love?

Next Week

Today we learned that holiness involves learning to love one another, and that this process requires that we prepare our minds to rid ourselves of wickedness. In the coming week, prayerfully seek to prepare your mind for action, taking stock of ways in which wickedness is part of your thinking. Next week we will be challenged even further, learning that we are holy priests who are to be set apart for service to God.

Notes on 1 Peter 1:13–2:3

SUMMARY: In this passage, Peter continues his discussion of who his readers are as the people of God. Their identity is not only derived from the fact of their salvation (1:3–12), but from the lifestyle that results from their experience of God's grace (1:13–25). This lifestyle involves three things: holiness (1:13–16), reverence (1:17–21), and love (1:22–25). Peter describes this lifestyle by means of a series of exhortations (1:13–15,17,22–23) based on Scripture (1:16,24–25) and on their experience (1:18–21). Peter moves from the great salvation they can look forward to in the future (1:3–12) to the battle of living that they face in the here and now (1:13–2:3).

1:13 *Therefore.* The salvation they have received results in a distinctive lifestyle involving clarity of mind, self-control and an active hope. Given the severity of their situation, they cannot afford to act without thought, in an extreme or undisciplined way, or on the basis of despair. *get your minds*

ready for action. This is the first of a series of imperatives (commands) in this passage. This phrase means literally "gird up the loins of your mind." It paints a picture of a man gathering up his long robe and tucking it in his belt ("girding up") so that he can run without hindrance. In order to live as they ought, they too must prepare themselves; specifically they need clarity of mind. They must think about how they live and not merely react. This is a time for cool heads and carefully thought-through actions.

1:14 *do not be conformed to the desires.* They are not to allow themselves to be shaped by the sensuality of their pre-Christian existence. They might be tempted to go along with the norms of others and not to stand out as different, thus escaping notice in the persecution. *ignorance.* Not only was their pre-Christian life dominated by physical desires of all sorts, they also lived in ignorance of God. Pagans in the first century believed in God, but thought him to be unknowable and uninterested in human beings.

1:15 *holy.* The holiness to which Peter calls them is not ritual in nature as it had become in Judaism, nor magical in content as it was in paganism.

1:16 *it is written.* Peter appeals to Scripture for his authority to urge such holiness on them.

1:17 God is both their Father and their Judge. On both counts their attitude ought to be one of "reverent fear." *reverence.* What Peter encourages here is not so much fear as it is awe. *temporary residence.* Christians are to make decisions not in terms of their present circumstances, but in the light of God's kingdom where their true home is found.

1:18 *For you know that.* Peter is referring to what they knew from creeds, catechism and liturgy. What Peter describes in the next few verses is the church's teaching on the redeeming work of Jesus. *redeemed.* To redeem someone is to rescue that person from bondage. This is a technical term for the money paid to buy freedom for a slave.

1:19 The price of their ransom from their pagan lifestyle was not material ("silver or gold") but spiritual (the "blood of Christ"). Here, Peter refers to Jesus in sacrificial terms as the innocent victim dying in place of others. *blood.* In the Old Testament, the blood of the sacrificial animal was offered to God in place of the life of the sinner. In the New Testament, it is not the sacrifice of animals that secures forgiveness; it is the death of Jesus who gave himself once for all. *without defect or blemish.* Jesus was able to be such a sacrifice because he was without sin. This is a remarkable confession from one like Peter who lived in close contact with Jesus for three years. Of all people, Peter would have been able to point out sin in Jesus' life, had there been any.

1:21 *who through Him are believers in God.* Yet another aspect of Christ's work: they came to belief in the true and living God via Jesus. In Jesus they saw and understood who God was. *raised Him from the dead and gave Him glory.* Jesus' redemptive work began with the Cross, but was not complete until he was resurrected and glorified. Crucifixion, resurrection, and glorification are all part of one event. *faith and hope.* Their faith (trust) and hope is that they, too, will share in the resurrection life of Jesus and in the glory that is his.

1:22 *obedience/purified.* Purification comes from obedience, and this issues in love for others. In the Old Testament, there was a ritual purification of objects and people so as to fit them for the service of God (Num. 8:21; 31:23). In the New Testament, purification is of a moral nature. Christians are called upon to rid themselves of those vices, passions, and negative attitudes (2:1) that make it difficult to love others. *sincere love.* The word Peter uses for love is *philadelphia* (not *agape*) and refers to love between Christian brothers and sisters.

1:23–25 Peter contrasts human and divine birth (perishable seed vs. imperishable seed) in order to explain the origin of this new community.

2:1 They are to rid themselves of all those behaviors which work against brotherly love. The list Peter uses here is similar to other such vice lists in the New Testament (Rom. 1:29–30; Eph. 4:31). *rid yourselves.* This verb was used to describe taking off one's clothes. They must strip off, like spoiled and dirty clothes, their old lifestyle. *all wickedness, all deceit.* These are general terms which refer to attitudes that disrupt a community. *hypocrisy, envy, and all slander.* Specific vices that make relationships difficult. Hypocrites pretend to be one thing while, in fact, they are concealing their true motives. Envy is jealousy of another's place and privilege. Slander involves speaking evil of others when they are not there to defend themselves.

2:2 Having rid themselves of the old ways, they are like newborn babies. They need pure milk which will nourish them so that they grow to maturity. *desire.* Having described them as newborn babies, he continues the metaphor by drawing upon the idea of the strong, natural, instinctive desire that infants have for milk. *unadulterated.* This is the first of two adjectives that describe the milk they are to crave. In Greek the word is *adolos* and it means "free from deceit." It is set in contrast to the deceit (*dolos*) they are to rid themselves of (2:1). *milk.* The milk to which Peter refers is the Word of God, which is supported by two other references in the New Testament (1 Cor. 3:2; Heb. 5:12–14). In both cases, religious instruction is referred to as "milk," and emphasizes that the source of teaching for Christians is the Scripture.

2:3 In the end, however, it is not words about Christ that sustain them; it is Christ himself. They have "tasted that the Lord is good" (Ps. 34:8).

Royal Priesthood

SCRIPTURE 1 PETER 2:4–12

Last Week

In our previous session, we learned that followers of Christ are to be holy, loving one another from pure hearts. This requires that we rid our lives of wickedness, envy, slander, deceit, hypocrisy—any form of sin against our brothers and sisters. This week we will consider how we are to be holy because we are called to be a royal priesthood, responsible for showing God's mercy to the world around us.

Ice-Breaker   15 Min.

CONNECT WITH YOUR GROUP

LEADER

Begin the session with a word of prayer. Welcome and introduce new group members. Choose one, two or all three of the Ice-Breaker questions.

Peter describes Jesus in our Scripture for today as the "living stone," upon which we should build our lives. When have you poured your heart and soul into building or creating something? Take turns sharing some of your thoughts and experiences with building things.

1. If you were able to build your dream house, what would it be like?

- ○ The Taj Mahal.
- ○ Abe Lincoln's cabin.
- ○ St. Paul's Cathedral.
- ○ A mansion in Newport.
- ○ The house in *The Waltons*.
- ○ Other _____.

2. Where would you live if you could make your wishes come true?

3. Have you ever fallen or nearly fallen from a great height? What happened?

READ SCRIPTURE AND DISCUSS

Have one group member, whom you have selected beforehand, read aloud the Scripture passage. Then discuss the Questions for Interaction, dividing into subgroups of three to six.

Paul now expands on his previous exhortations, teaching us that we are actually a "royal priesthood"— people who have been set apart by God to intercede for those around us, teaching by example of the grace and mercy of God. Read 1 Peter 2:4–12, and note how only with Jesus as our cornerstone can we live a holy life.

A Royal Priesthood

4Coming to Him, a living stone—rejected by men but chosen and valuable to God— 5you yourselves, as living stones, are being built into a spiritual house for a holy priesthood to offer spiritual sacrifices acceptable to God through Jesus Christ. 6For it stands in Scripture:

> "Look! I lay a stone in Zion,
> a chosen and valuable cornerstone,
> and the one who believes in Him
> will never be put to shame!"

7So the honor is for you who believe; but for the unbelieving,

> "The stone that the builders rejected—
> this One has become the cornerstone,"

and

> 8"A stone that causes men to stumble,
> and a rock that trips them up."

They stumble by disobeying the message; they were destined for this.

> 9But you are a chosen race, a royal priesthood,
> a holy nation, a people for His possession,
> so that you may proclaim the praises
> of the One who called you out of darkness
> into His marvelous light.
> 10Once you were not a people,
> but now you are God's people;
> you had not received mercy,
> but now you have received mercy.

11Dear friends, I urge you as aliens and temporary residents to abstain from fleshly desires that war against you. 12Conduct yourselves honorably among the Gentiles, so that in a case where they speak against you as those who do evil, they may, by observing your good works, glorify God in a day of visitation.

1 Peter 2:4–12

QUESTIONS FOR INTERACTION

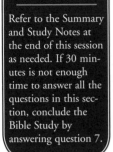

Refer to the Summary and Study Notes at the end of this session as needed. If 30 minutes is not enough time to answer all the questions in this section, conclude the Bible Study by answering question 7.

1. What sort of "spiritual house" have you been in this past week, and why?

○ Cabin.
○ Mansion.
○ Cathedral.
○ Tent.
○ Igloo.
○ Other _____.

2. What does it mean that Christ is a "living stone" (v. 4)?

3. What are the implications for our own lives that we also are living stones?

4. How can Jesus be both a "cornerstone" and a "stone that causes men to stumble" (vv. 7–8)? How does Jesus "trip people up" today?

5. What are the implications of knowing that you are chosen by God—that you belong to him (vv. 9–10)?

6. If we are actually "a chosen race, a royal priesthood, a holy nation" how should we be living our lives? How should we interact with the people around us?

7. What sort of "fleshly desires" are at war against you right now? What effect is this war having on your "spiritual house?"

GOING DEEPER:

If your group has time and/or wants a challenge, go on to this question.

8. Why are Christians called a royal priesthood? What implications does this "royalty" have in our daily lives?

Caring Time
15 Min.

APPLY THE LESSON AND PRAY FOR ONE ANOTHER

LEADER

Be sure to save at least 15 minutes for this important time. After sharing together from the following questions and asking for prayer requests, end in a time of group prayer. Pray especially that the Lord will lead group members to others who do not know the Gospel.

Once again, take some time now to encourage one another in your faith by discussing the following questions and sharing prayer requests.

1. Where are you in the journey of following Christ, the cornerstone?

○ I am a seeker.
○ I have just begun the journey.
○ I'm returning after getting lost on the wrong path.
○ I've been following Christ for a long time.
○ Other _____.

2. How can the group pray for you as you struggle against "fleshly desires?"

3. In what practical ways can this group be a priesthood to those in our lives who don't know Christ?

Next Week

Today we learned that the calling of the Christian is to proclaim the Good News of God's grace to the world around us, particularly by example, living lives that resist the fleshly desires of the world. In the coming week, seek to be a priest who intercedes for and loves those around you. Work at not becoming a stumbling block by abstaining from sinful desires. Next week we will learn that this role also involves humble submission to those in authority over us.

SUMMARY: Thus far Peter has pointed out two things about the identity of the people of God: (1) who they are is grounded in their experience of salvation (1:3–12), and (2) who they are is expressed in the kind of life they lead (1:13–2:3). Here he adds a third point: they have a special task. He uses two metaphors to describe this role: (1) they are living stones who are being built up into a spiritual house (vv. 4–8), and (2) they are a royal priesthood who declare the praises of God (vv. 9–12). As in the previous passage, Peter begins and ends with exhortations (vv. 4–5,11–12) and he bases his appeals on Scripture.

2:4 *Coming to Him.* Here Peter pictures them coming to the Lord—though he changes his metaphor. Now Jesus is the living Stone. In verse 5 he tells them what will happen as they come: they will become a spiritual house in which they serve God as a holy priesthood. This verb is used in the Old Testament for coming to God in worship. *a living Stone.* Peter shifts his description of Jesus from the "lamb without blemish" (1:19) to the "living Stone." He gets this metaphor from two Old Testament texts: Isaiah 28:16 (v. 6) speaks of "a chosen and precious cornerstone" and Psalm 118:22 (v. 7) speaks of the rejection of that stone. Both verses point out the supreme value of the cornerstone. Peter's point is that, despite his rejection, Christ is the chosen one of God, and in the end he prevails. *living.* An allusion to Christ's resurrection (1:3, 21). He is alive and able to give his resurrection life to those who come to him. *chosen.* Peter has already made the point that they have been chosen by God and he will make the same point again (v. 9). Here he adds to this the fact that Jesus was also chosen by God. Furthermore, this fact was not accepted. People rejected Jesus. In like manner, this will be their experience; they will be chosen but rejected. *valuable.* People may reject Jesus, but God gives him great honor.

2:5 *you yourselves, as living stones.* So close is the relationship between Christians and Christ that Peter uses the same metaphor to describe both. The implication is that these Christians (like Christ) will know rejection and triumph. *being built into.* Stones by themselves serve no function. But shaped together into a structure by a master builder, they become something of use and importance. *a spiritual house.* Peter shifts from a biological image ("newborn babies"—2:2) to an architectural one. They are a "spiritual house." As living stones they have been built into a holy temple. The church is the temple of God, made up of a close-knit community of men and women. Here is where God dwells, in contrast to temples built by human hands. *a holy priesthood.* Peter shifts the metaphor again. Not only are they a "spiritual house," they are the priests who serve in it! Priests were common figures in the first-century world. Their function was to mediate between God and the people. Typically, they were members of a special caste; priests were privileged and set apart. But no such elitism exists in the church. All Christians are members of this royal priesthood. *offer spiritual sacrifices.* The function of priests was to offer sacrifices of animals, grain, wine, etc. The sacrifice of Christians, however, is spiritual, not material, because Christ's great sacrifice of himself for the sins of the world was the ultimate and final sacrifice. What these New Testament priests can offer to God is love, faith, surrender, service, prayer, thanksgiving, sharing, etc. They offer lives that bring praise (Rom. 12:1; Eph. 5:1–2; Phil. 4:18; Heb. 13:15–16). Their sacrifice is also "spiritual" in the sense that it is inspired by the Spirit. *acceptable to God through Jesus Christ.* All their efforts, however, would fail to satisfy God were it not for the sacrifice already made by Jesus himself.

2:6 In its original context, Isaiah was speaking to the leaders of Israel who had just made a pact with Egypt, in response to the threat of an invasion by Assyria. Isaiah points to the solid temple as an illustration of where their true strength lies. They need to trust God, not alliances. Later, rabbis understood this reference to the cornerstone to be a description of the Messiah whom God would establish in Zion.

2:7 In Psalm 118:22, the stone stood for Israel, which the world powers considered useless and which they threw away. However, God gave Israel the most important place in building his kingdom. This text was taken by the early church to be a prophecy of Jesus' rejection and death by the powers-that-be and his subsequent vindication by God as demonstrated in his resurrection and glorification (Acts 4:8–12). This interpretation came from Jesus, who spoke about himself in these terms (Mark 12:10).

2:8 *disobeying.* Just as Peter's readers are characterized by their "obedience to Jesus Christ" (1:2), others are characterized by disobedience. *destined for.* Those who have obeyed are chosen and destined for a glorious inheritance. Those who have stumbled over Christ have a different destiny.

2:9–10 In contrast to the destiny of their persecutors, they have a fine destiny. Peter lists a series of titles drawn from the Old Testament (primarily from Ex. 19:5–6 and Isa. 43:20–21), which once were applied to Israel, but now belong to them.

2:9 *a chosen race.* Just as Jesus is "chosen by God" (v. 4), so too are they as his people (1:1–2). *a holy nation.* The church is the true Israel, the heir of all the promises and privileges of the old Israel. *a people for His possession.* The church is a community chosen by God. *that you may proclaim the praises of the One.* This is their role. This is what their "spiritual sacrifices" are all about: they are to make God known in the world. In verses 11–12 he spells out what this means.

2:10 Peter contrasts what they have become with what they once were. This time he draws his language from Hosea (Hos. 1:6,9; 2:23). The names applied to these Christians are the names God directed Hosea to give to the children born of Gomer.

2:11 *aliens and temporary residents.* They may be a chosen nation and a royal priesthood, but they are also outsiders in terms of the world in which they live. *abstain from fleshly desires.* "Fleshly desires" is literally "fleshly lusts." It is translated as it is here in order to convey its real meaning since "fleshly lusts" is a phrase that has come to stand for sexual sin. However, in the New Testament sins of the flesh encompass a far wider sphere than sexuality, including such things as pride, envy, hatred, etc. (Gal. 5:19–21 for a representative list).

SESSION 5
Submit Yourselves
SCRIPTURE 1 PETER 2:13-25

Last Week

Looking to Jesus as our "living stone" and being God's chosen people were two ideas we discussed in last week's session. We were reminded that, as a royal priesthood, we are responsible to show forth the grace and mercy of God to the world around us by living holy lives. This week we will consider how this role also requires our submission to the authorities that God has placed in our lives.

Ice-Breaker   15 Min.

CONNECT WITH YOUR GROUP

LEADER

Open with a word of prayer, and then introduce any new people or visitors. Have your group members take turns sharing their responses to one, two or all three of the Ice-Breaker questions. Be sure that everyone gets a chance to participate.

We've all heard the expression, "you can't escape death or taxes." When we talk about submission, these are two areas of life about which we don't like to be reminded. Take turns sharing your thoughts and experiences with submission to difficult situations in your life.

1. How do you feel about the taxes withheld from your paycheck?

○ They should take more.
○ It's just about right.
○ They should take less.
○ They should not take anything!
○ Other _____.

2 What was your first "real" job? What was your boss like?

3. As a teenager, what authority figure did you have the most run-ins with?

READ SCRIPTURE AND DISCUSS

LEADER

Ask two group members, whom you have selected beforehand, to read aloud the Scripture passage. Assign the readings as outlined. Then discuss the Questions for Interaction, dividing into sub-groups of three to six.

Peter now becomes more specific in his instructions on holiness, teaching us that all believers must submit to all human authorities, even to cruel masters. This would have been especially hard for Christians to hear who were suffering life-threatening persecution. Read 1 Peter 2:13–25, and note how Peter reminds us that we are only imitating Christ himself, who submitted to the point of death for us on the cross.

Submission to Rulers and Masters

Reader One: ¹³Submit to every human institution because of the Lord, whether to the Emperor as the supreme authority, ¹⁴or to governors as those sent out by him to punish those who do evil and to praise those who do good. ¹⁵For it is God's will that you, by doing good, silence the ignorance of foolish people. ¹⁶As God's slaves, live as free people, but don't use your freedom as a way to conceal evil. ¹⁷Honor everyone. Love the brotherhood. Fear God. Honor the Emperor.

Reader Two: ¹⁸Household slaves, submit yourselves to your masters with all respect, not only to the good and gentle but also to the cruel. ¹⁹For it brings favor if, because of conscience toward God, someone endures grief from suffering unjustly. ²⁰For what credit is there if you endure when you sin and are beaten? But when you do good and suffer, if you endure, it brings favor with God.

> ²¹For you were called to this,
>   because Christ also suffered for you,
>   leaving you an example,
>   so that you should follow in His steps.
> ²²"He did not commit sin,
>   and no deceit was found in His mouth;"
> ²³when reviled, He did not revile in return;
>   when suffering, He did not threaten,
>   but committed Himself to the One who judges justly.
> ²⁴He Himself bore our sins
>   in His body on the tree,
>   so that, having died to sins,
>   we might live for righteousness;
>   by His wounding you have been healed.
> ²⁵For you were like sheep going astray,
>   but you have now returned
>   to the shepherd and guardian of your souls.

1 Peter 2:13–25

QUESTIONS FOR INTERACTION

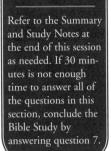

Refer to the Summary and Study Notes at the end of this session as needed. If 30 minutes is not enough time to answer all of the questions in this section, conclude the Bible Study by answering question 7.

1. Which of the following "human institutions" is a Christian to submit to?

- ○ Federal government.
- ○ State government.
- ○ Local government.
- ○ Police.
- ○ Employer.
- ○ Other _____.

2 How does "doing good" silence the "ignorance of foolish people" (v. 15)? Who are these foolish people?

3. How would the example of Christ have helped the Christians suffering under Nero? How can it help us today?

4. We do not retain "household slaves" in our culture. How might verse 18 apply to us today?

5. What is to be our motive when we submit to unjust suffering? How does this bring favor with God?

6. Have you ever suffered under a "cruel master" (v. 18)? How did you respond?

7. To whom do you need to submit yourself more fully in the coming week? In what way can you do this?

GOING DEEPER:

If your group has time and/or wants a challenge, go on to this question.

8. How can a Christian live as a free person if he is God's slave (v. 16)?

Caring Time   15 Min.

APPLY THE LESSON AND PRAY FOR ONE ANOTHER

LEADER

Encourage everyone to participate in this important time and be sure that each group member is receiving prayer support. Continue to pray for the empty chair in the closing group prayer.

Most of us, at one time or another, have suffered from a cruel boss or from the taunts of "foolish people." Take some time to support and encourage those in the group who are experiencing any of these struggles this week.

1. Have you been tempted to "use your freedom as a way to conceal evil" recently? How will you resist the temptation in the future?

2. What concerns do you have about your job and the work you do?

3. Are you struggling with "foolish people" at present? Are you suffering unjustly? How can the group pray for you?

Next Week

In our study this week we considered several topics: (1) Christians are to submit to all authorities, even those that are unjust or cruel; (2) we are to imitate Christ in the way that he submitted to injustice and mockery; and (3) we are to guard against the temptation to use our spiritual freedoms to conceal evil. In the coming week, allow the Holy Spirit to address these topics in your own life, praying that he will help you to imitate the example of Jesus. Next week we will bring this subject even closer to home, as we consider the mutual submission of husbands and wives.

Notes on 1 Peter 2:13–25

SUMMARY: In the first part of his letter, Peter deals with the identity of the people of God (1:1–2:12). In the second part, which begins with this passage, he looks at the responsibilities of the people of God (2:13–4:11). Here in this section, he begins his discussion of lifestyle by counseling them to adopt an attitude of respect. He starts by urging respect for everyone (vv. 13–17), with a special look at civil authorities. He then goes on to urge slaves to respect their masters (vv. 18–25).

2:13–17 Peter begins by counseling respect for all people. Although special attention is focused on rulers, the call is general in nature: "Honor everyone" (v. 17). They are to do this "because of the Lord" (v. 13) and because they are "God's slaves" (v. 16).

2:13 *Submit.* This is the key concept in the next two passages. What Peter urges is voluntary subordination in all spheres of human life. When the verb "submit" is used in the New Testament, it is voluntary in nature (e.g., "submit yourself"). The call is never to make others submit to you. We are to "yield to," "adapt to," "give way to" others. *to every human institution.* This phrase literally means "every human creature." Understanding the phrase this way reinforces the generalized nature of this call which is spelled out clearly in verse 17: "Honor everyone."

2:13–14 *Emperor/governors.* The first situation in which Peter applies this general principle is with civil authorities. Peter's instructions here are quite similar to those of Paul in Romans 13:1–7 and Jesus in Matthew 22:21. The New Testament counsels Christians to be model citizens of the country they inhabit.

2:14 *punish/praise.* The role of these authorities is to prevent crime and suppress injustice. How they "praise those who do good" is not clear, though what Peter may mean by this is that governments tend to look with favor on law-abiding citizens, which is what Peter is urging these Asian Christians to be.

2:15 These Christians were, apparently, subject to slander ("ignorant talk") on the part of people who did not really know what was going on ("foolish people"). ***ignorance.*** The Greek word used here suggests willful ignorance, the unwillingness to find out what is really true.

2:16 Christ brought new freedom to men and women who had long been bound by rules and regulations. While affirming this newfound freedom, Peter cautions that they must not let their liberty degenerate into license. ***God's slaves.*** The paradox is that Christians are both free and bound. They are to "live as free people" while simultaneously they are "God's slaves."

2:17 Peter gives two pairs of commands here. The inclusiveness of "everyone" is balanced by the more focused concern for the "brotherhood." Likewise, the local authority of the king is set in the context of the overarching authority of God. ***Love the brotherhood.*** While respect is to be shown to all, it is necessary to go beyond respect to love when it comes to one's fellow Christians. ***Fear God.*** The respect due God is, in fact, the "reverent fear" that Peter has already talked about in 1:17. ***Honor the Emperor.*** The kind of respect due the king is of a different sort. The word "fear" has religious connotations while "honor" is a secular term. This too was an amazing injunction. The king was the one

responsible for the persecution they were experiencing.

2:18 *slaves, submit yourselves.* Slaves were the legal property of their masters. This fact defined the reality within which Peter's audience had to live. Peter and other New Testament writers do not counsel rebellion or even "passive resistance." What gave slaves the freedom to submit in this way is the sense that they as Christians were, in fact, members of a heavenly family and of a kingdom far more significant than the earthly reality within which they lived. Indeed, when the Lord returns their true position will be revealed and they will live in this new reality for the age to come. ***with all respect.*** This phrase is literally, "with all fear." This is not, however, fear toward the master (Peter rejects such a posture in 3:14) but reverence toward God who is their true Master (vv. 16–17).

2:19 *grief from suffering unjustly.* It was not easy to be a slave. Slaves were considered to be property and therefore their owners had absolute control over them.

2:21–25 Jesus is their model for the way to act in the face of injustice. Here, Peter is probably quoting from or alluding to an ancient creed, hymn, or liturgy. This whole section echoes Isaiah 52:13–53:12.

2:21 *For you were called to this, because Christ also suffered for you.* The basis on which Peter says what he does about accepting unjust treatment is the example of Jesus who suffered for mankind. Christian slaves are to imitate Christ.

2:22 Peter directly quotes Isaiah 53:9 to point out once again the sinlessness of Jesus (1:19). A slave would understand that innocence was no guarantee of just treatment.

2:24 In a key passage about the atonement, Peter points out that Jesus was their representative. He bore their sins. He took upon himself the penalty which they deserved because of their sin. ***tree.*** This is literally "wood" and was used both in the Old Testament (Deut. 21:23) and New Testament

(Acts 5:30; Gal. 3:13) to refer to a means of punishment. *so that.* Peter points to two results of Jesus' death on the cross: (1) because of it we are able to die to sin; and (2) we can now live for righteousness. In other words, it is the moral impact of the Cross which Peter chooses to highlight here, and not the forgiveness of sin or remission of guilt which are also the result of the atonement. The death of Jesus makes it possible for us to leave our old lives of sin and follow instead a new way of life. *wounding.* The Greek word refers to the welts and swelling which result from blows to the body with a fist or a whip. *healed.* Christ's wounds brought restoration to our sin-scarred lives.

2:25 *returned.* We were once like lost sheep, but now we have been converted—turned around and come back to Christ. *shepherd.* This was a common Old Testament image: God was like a Shepherd calling together his wandering sheep. In the New Testament this title was applied to Jesus.

SESSION 6
Wives and Husbands
SCRIPTURE 1 PETER 3:1—7

Last Week

In last week's session, we were reminded by Peter that we are to submit to authority, even when that authority is unjust or cruel. We are to look to Christ as our example, as he submitted even to death on the cross for our salvation. This week Peter brings the subject of submission much closer to home—wives are to submit to their husbands, and husbands are to honor their wives.

Ice-Breaker   15 Min.

CONNECT WITH YOUR GROUP

LEADER

Begin the session with a word of prayer. Have your group members take turns sharing their responses to one, two or all three of the Ice-Breaker questions. Remember to stick closely to the three-part agenda and the time allowed for each segment.

Beauty, they say, is in the eye of the beholder. The definition of beauty in today's culture is a bit different from Peter's definition in today's passage. Take turns sharing some of your thoughts about beauty and marriage.

1. Who is the most beautiful person you can think of?

- ○ A famous model.
- ○ A high-profile celebrity.
- ○ My mom.
- ○ My spouse.
- ○ Other _____.

2 What is your favorite piece of jewelry or clothes to wear, and why?

- ○ Wedding ring.
- ○ Heirloom brooch.
- ○ Class ring.
- ○ Sentimental necklace.
- ○ Fur coat.
- ○ Designer watch.
- ○ Silk necktie.
- ○ My team jersey or jacket.
- ○ Other _____.

3. If married, what is something that you really appreciate about your spouse?

- ○ Close friendship.
- ○ Steadfast loyalty.
- ○ Gentle compassion.
- ○ Understanding.
- ○ Respect.
- ○ Other _____.

Bible Study   30 Min.

READ SCRIPTURE AND DISCUSS

LEADER

Have two group members, whom you have selected beforehand, read aloud the Scripture passage. Then discuss the Questions for Interaction, dividing into subgroups of three to six.

Paul now continues on his subject of submission, this time bringing it right into our homes. The topic of submission is very volatile in our society, especially when applied to women. We must approach our study of Scripture with the attitude that, when it collides with culture, it is culture that is wrong, not Scripture. Peter tells us that wives are to submit to their husbands, and husbands are to respect and honor their wives. The fact that he pinpoints different commands for each partner suggests that those attitudes might not come naturally. Read 1 Peter 3:1–7, and note how true beauty is described.

Wives and Husbands

Reader One: 3 Wives, in the same way, submit yourselves to your own husbands so that, even if some disobey the Christian message, they may be won over without a message by the way their wives live, ²when they observe your pure, reverent lives. ³Your beauty should not consist of outward things like elaborate hairstyles and the wearing of gold ornaments or fine clothes; ⁴instead, it should consist of the hidden person of the heart with the imperishable quality of a gentle and quiet spirit, which is very valuable in God's eyes. ⁵For in the past, the holy women who hoped in God also beautified themselves in this way, submitting to their own husbands, ⁶just as Sarah obeyed Abraham, calling him lord. You have become her children when you do good and aren't frightened by anything alarming.

Reader Two: ⁷Husbands, in the same way, live with your wives with understanding of their weaker nature yet showing them honor as co-heirs of the grace of life, so that your prayers will not be hindered.

1 Peter 3:1–7

QUESTIONS FOR INTERACTION

LEADER

Refer to the Summary and Study Notes at the end of this session as needed. If 30 minutes is not enough time to answer all of the questions in this section, conclude the Bible Study by answering question 8.

1. What is your short definition of a good marriage?

- ○ A spiritual team.
- ○ A safe harbor.
- ○ A lifetime of friendship.
- ○ A fun partnership.
- ○ Other _____.

2. Who is the happiest married couple you know? What is the secret of their success?

3. Why are wives to submit to their husbands? According to the passage, what does this submission entail?

4. What is to be the source of a wife's beauty? Why does Peter apply this particularly to women? Might the same principle apply to husbands as well?

5. What powerful impact can a submissive spirit have on an unbelieving spouse?

6. Why are husbands commanded to be understanding of their wife's "weaker nature?" What exactly does Peter mean by this phrase?

7. Why are husbands specifically commanded to live with their wife?

8. How does a husband show his wife honor, in practical terms?

GOING DEEPER:

If your group has time and/or wants a challenge, go on to this question.

9. In what way will a man's prayers be "hindered" (v. 7) if he fails to treat his wife properly?

Caring Time   15 Min.

APPLY THE LESSON AND PRAY FOR ONE ANOTHER

LEADER

Be sure to save at least 15 minutes for this time of prayer and encouragement. Continue to encourage group members to invite new people to the group. Remind them that this group is for learning and sharing, but also for reaching out to others.

Knowing that God wants us to love one another earnestly and with a pure heart, come before him now and support one another with a time of sharing and prayer. Encourage each other to focus on obeying what God has decreed as our responsibilities to one another.

1. How are you doing in your own marriage? Are you obeying the commands given in this passage?

2. If you are single, how can you prepare now to become the sort of husband or wife that Peter describes?

3. If you are married, how can this group be supportive to your marriage? What prayers do you especially need right now?

Next Week

Today we examined some challenging teaching, requiring that husbands and wives live together in godliness, submission, respect and love. This week, ask the Lord to show you ways in which you can become a better husband or wife. If you are not married, ask the Lord to show you how to love and honor him in an even deeper way. Next week we will address the fact that sometimes Christians can suffer when trying to do what is right.

Notes on 1 Peter 3:1–7

SUMMARY: Peter continues his discussion of relationships. His general principle is "respect for all," and thus far he has shown how this applies to the relationship between Christians and secular rulers and between Christian slaves and their masters. In this passage, he looks at how wives and husbands are to relate to each other. Here Peter tells wives to respect their husbands (vv. 1–6) and husbands to respect their wives (v. 7). His particular concern is with Christian wives who have pagan husbands (vv. 1–4). What he says is based on principles drawn from the Old Testament (vv. 5–6).

3:1 *in the same way.* By this phrase Peter makes a transition from Christ's example (at the end of chapter 2) to wives. Just as the behavior of Christ was the model for submitting to all earthly authority, so too is it for women. *submit yourselves.* Peter counsels submission, not rebellion. *even if some disobey.* Just as we are to submit to "masters" who might be cruel (2:18), Peter coun-

sels wives to submit to their husbands whether or not they obey the commands of God. *won over.* Peter (like Paul) does not counsel Christian women to leave pagan husbands. His desire is that the husbands be converted. So he describes the kind of attitude and behavior on the part of the wife that has the potential to lead an unbelieving husband to faith.

3:2 *pure, reverent lives.* What the pagan husband will notice about his wife is how she lives now that she has become a Christian. In particular, he will note her "purity." This word refers not just to sexual purity (chaste behavior), but also to purity of thought, motive, and action. He will see her "reverence," that she has an awareness of God that causes her to live a good life.

3:3 *outward things.* Whether women should spend so much time and energy on clothes and jewelry was a question of some debate in the first century. What Peter says here finds its root in the Old Testament; for example, Isa. 3:18–24 lists various forms of adornment and comments that all this will pass away on the Day of Judgment.

3:5 *holy women.* They were "holy" not in the sense of being pious, but because they were chosen by God for his purposes.

3:6 *Sarah.* The point of Peter's reference to Sarah is that wives in the new covenant can learn from their spiritual ancestress. If Sarah submitted in obedience, her spiritual daughters ought also to submit in servanthood. Sarah called Abraham "lord," but Christian wives are never told to call their husbands "lord" anywhere in the Bible. Instead, they are told in this verse to not give way to fear. "There is no fear in love; instead, perfect love drives out fear" (1 John 4:18).

3:7 Peter reminds husbands that the respect they are to show to all people (2:17) is also due to their own wives. Both Peter and Paul make a point of identifying the obligations of a husband to a wife (Eph. 5:25–33). *in the same way.* As he did when he addressed wives (v. 1), here too, in addressing husbands, Peter harkens back to the example of Christ who voluntarily gave himself for the sake of others (2:21). *with understanding.* The phrase means literally "live with them according to knowledge." By "knowledge" is meant having a conscience sensitive to God's will. *their weaker nature.* Literally, the "weaker vessel." There has been much debate as to what this means. It might refer to anatomical differences between men and women (this phrase was used in Greek to refer to the woman's body), to the inferior position of women in that society, or to the comparative lack of physical strength on the part of the woman. By Peter's own example, it cannot mean inferiority spiritually or morally. His wife accompanied him on his preaching tours (1 Cor. 9:5) and according to a reliable tradition she joined him in death as a martyr. *co-heirs of the grace of life.* Both husband and wife are equal participants in the grace of God, again reinforcing the idea of the new mutuality that has come to men and women who are in Christ.

SESSION 7

Suffering for Doing Good
SCRIPTURE 1 PETER 3:8-22

 ## Last Week

In last week's session, we discussed the proper way for husbands and wives to love one another. We were also reminded of the true definition of beauty, which is the opposite of popular culture's definition. This week we will learn how we can come to love life, and how we can share with others the love for God that is within us.

Ice-Breaker   15 Min.

CONNECT WITH YOUR GROUP

LEADER

Begin the session with a word of prayer, and then introduce and welcome any new group members or visitors. Have your group members take turns sharing their responses to one, two or all three of the Ice-Breaker questions. Be sure that everyone gets a chance to participate.

Suffering can come in many forms, but it is especially difficult when it's for doing good. Many people fear suffering so much that it can keep them from accomplishing God's purpose for their lives. Take turns sharing about suffering and fear in your life.

1. What is something that you are afraid of?

- ○ Spiders.
- ○ Snakes.
- ○ Flying.
- ○ Heights.
- ○ Small spaces.
- ○ Big spaces.
- ○ Speaking in public.
- ○ Other _____.

2. Who is usually the peacemaker in your family?

3. If you've been baptized, when was it and where?

Bible Study   30 Min.

READ SCRIPTURE AND DISCUSS

LEADER

Have two group members, whom you have selected before-hand, read aloud the Scripture passage. Assign the readings as outlined. Then discuss the Questions for Interaction, dividing into sub-groups of three to six.

Peter now shares with us a grand secret—the way in which we can come to love life and see good days. But he tempers this with the recognition that following Christ often includes suffering, even suffering for doing good. This knowledge, however, brings comfort and encouragement, because Jesus himself suffered for doing good and now sits at God's right hand.

Read 1 Peter 3:8–22, and note how true happiness is to be found.

Suffering for Doing Good

Reader One: ⁸Now finally, all of you should be like-minded and sympathetic, should love believers, and be compassionate and humble, ⁹not paying back evil for evil or insult for insult but, on the contrary, giving a blessing, since you were called for this, so that you can inherit a blessing.

> ¹⁰For "the one who wants to love life
> and to see good days
> must keep his tongue from evil
> and his lips from speaking deceit
> ¹¹and he must turn away from evil and do good.
> He must seek peace and pursue it
> ¹²because the eyes of the Lord are on the righteous
> and His ears are open to their request.
> But the face of the Lord is against those who do evil."

¹³And who will harm you if you are passionate for what is good? ¹⁴But even if you should suffer for righteousness, you are blessed. "Do not fear what they fear or be disturbed," ¹⁵but set apart the Messiah as Lord in your hearts, and always be ready to give a defense to anyone who asks you for a reason for the hope that is in you. ¹⁶However, do this with gentleness and respect, keeping your conscience clear, so that when you are accused, those who denounce your Christian life will be put to shame. ¹⁷For it is better to suffer for doing good, if that should be God's will, than for doing evil.

Reader Two: ¹⁸For Christ also suffered for sins once for all,

> the righteous for the unrighteous,
> that He might bring you to God,
> after being put to death in the fleshly realm
> but made alive in the spiritual realm.

¹⁹In that state He also went and made a proclamation to the spirits in prison ²⁰who in the past were disobedient, when God patiently waited in the days of Noah while an ark was being prepared; in it, a few—that is, eight people—were saved through water. ²¹Baptism, which corresponds to this, now saves you (not the removal of the filth of the flesh, but the pledge of a good conscience toward God) through the resurrection of Jesus Christ. ²²Now that He has gone into heaven, He is at God's right hand, with angels, authorities, and powers subjected to Him.

1 Peter 3:8–22

QUESTIONS FOR INTERACTION

Refer to the Summary and Study Notes at the end of this session as needed. If 30 minutes is not enough time to answer all of the questions in this section, conclude the Bible Study by answering question 7.

1. Share something really good that has happened to you lately.

2. What must one do to "love life and to see good days" (v. 10)? How can we do these things in practical terms?

3. What exactly is "the hope that is in you" (v. 15)? How can we be ready to "give a defense" for it?

4. In what way are we to tell others about the hope that Christ offers?

5. How does baptism correspond to Noah and the ark? What is the symbolism of baptism?

6. Peter states that Jesus was "put to death in the fleshly realm but made alive in the spiritual realm" (v. 18). How can this insight help you when you are suffering for doing good?

7. When have you had the opportunity of "giving a blessing" (v. 9) when you received evil or insult? How well did you do? What effect did it have?

GOING DEEPER:

If your group has time and/or wants a challenge, go on to this question.

8. What does Peter mean when he says that "baptism ... now saves you" (v. 21)?

Caring Time   15 Min.

APPLY THE LESSON AND PRAY FOR ONE ANOTHER

LEADER

Continue to encourage group members to invite new people to the group. Close the group prayer by thanking God for each member and for this time together.

It can be very difficult at times to "love life" simply because we do not always "see good days." Peter acknowledges this, warning us that following Christ often includes suffering for doing what is right. Encourage one another through sharing and prayer, whether you are enjoying life or suffering.

1. Do you know any non-Christians who are afraid or disturbed? How can you share the hope that is in you?

2 Are you suffering lately for doing good? How can the group support you?

3. How are you doing in the process of loving life and seeing good days?

Next Week

In this study, we learned the secret of how to enjoy life, while also finding encouragement for enduring those times when suffering does come. In the coming week, if you are suffering, consider the ways in which Jesus himself suffered for you, and pray that the Holy Spirit will strengthen you to be faithful. Consider the things involved in learning to love life, and ask for help in making them part of your life this week. Next week we will consider some very practical ways in which we can strengthen and encourage one another.

Notes on 1 Peter 3:8–22

SUMMARY: In the first paragraph of this passage (vv. 8–12) Peter concludes his comments on the nature of a missionary lifestyle. The question he has been dealing with is how we can "Conduct yourselves honorably among the Gentiles, so that in a case where they speak against you as those who do evil, they may, by observing your good works, glorify God in a day of visitation" (2:12). His answer in that respect is the key to this kind of lifestyle. Here in verses 8–12, by way of conclusion, he reiterates what he said in 2:17—respect both fellow believers (v. 8) and those who are your enemies (v. 9). In the second paragraph of this passage (vv. 13–22), Peter moves from urging respect for those who do evil to the evil itself, which is being done to the Christians in Asia. He talks about suffering for doing good (vv. 13–17) and about Christ as an example.

3:8–12 Peter ends his comments (begun back in 2:13) with some general advice concerning how they are to relate to one another and to the pagan community.

3:8 By means of five exhortations Peter defines how we as Christians ought to treat each other. *be like-minded.* The phrase is literally "all of one mind." By it Peter encourages the kind of unity that is vital in a hostile environment. There must be no divisions within the church. *sympathetic.* They must also be able to enter into and share the feelings of others. *love believers.* Peter uses the verb related to *philadelphia* (love amongst kin) instead of the more common verb related to *agape* (self-giving love). By it he encourages them to hold on to the kind of love that has knit them together as the family of Christ. *be compassionate.* The Greek word used here is derived from the word for heart, kidney, and liver—the internal organs. The Greeks thought these were the source of feelings. Peter is urging them to enter into the sufferings of others in their community with deep human emotion. *humble.* This was not a virtue much prized by the Greeks. Humility was for slaves and as such was despised. However, the humility of Jesus (who had all power and voluntarily gave it up) became the model for Christians, so in the church humility came to be seen in a positive light.

3:9 Peter tells us not to retaliate against those who persecute us. *blessing.* Instead, we are to bless our persecutors. This reinforces the advice he has given in the rest of this section. We are to act in unexpected ways.

3:10–12 Once again Peter refers back to Psalm 34 (2:3), where the theme is that the Lord will rescue his suffering children who trust in him.

3:13–17 Having pointed out how we are to relate to those who oppress us, now Peter looks directly at the oppression itself and how they are to respond to it. He reassures us that, in the end, righteous behavior will be vindicated. Even if we are persecuted, we are not to fear. Instead, we must focus inwardly on Jesus while outwardly displaying good behavior.

3:14 *But.* Peter does not mislead us, however. There is no assurance that good behavior will invariably shield us from harm. *blessed.* If we do suffer, rather than being downcast, we should count this as a privilege. *Do not fear.* Quoting Isaiah 8:12, Peter points out that the real danger is fear. "Do not fear what they fear" could also be translated, "Do not fear their threats."

3:15 *but.* Instead of fear in our hearts, we need to place Jesus there. *set apart the Messiah.* Literally, "sanctify" Christ. Christ is to be acknowledged as holy and worshiped as Lord. We are to open ourselves to his inner presence. *in your hearts.* At the core of our being Christ must reign. *be ready to give a defense.* Although this may refer to an official inquiry in which we are called upon to defend the fact that we are Christians, it probably is more general in reference. When anybody asks about the hope we have, we are to explain why we are followers of Jesus. *a reason.* Greeks valued a logical, intelligent statement as to why one held certain beliefs.

3:16 *with gentleness and respect.* This reply should not be given in a contentious or defensive way. *keeping your conscience clear.* The inner awareness of what is right morally. If we are living in the way Peter describes, we will have nothing to hide; there will be no guilt to make us defensive.

3:18–22 The reason why we can be so confident in the face of suffering is that Christ has won the victory over death. Furthermore, if we do suffer, we are simply walking the same path as our Lord.

3:18 *suffered for sins.* Christ died—as have men and women down through the ages. But his death was different in that it was a full, sufficient, and adequate sacrifice that atones for the sins of all people. *once for all.* The sacrifices in the temple had to be repeated over and over again; Christ's sacrifice was the final and perfect sacrifice through which all people in all ages find salvation. *the righteous for the unrighteous.* His death was vicarious—he died in the place of others. *bring you to God.* It is because of Christ's death that we are restored to a right relationship with God.

3:19 *made a proclamation.* The nature of Jesus' proclamation has been interpreted as: (1) the Gospel which is proclaimed to those who lived before Christ came, or as (2) the announcement to the rebellious spirits that their power has been broken. *the spirits.* Who these spirits are is not clear. They have been variously identified as: (1) sinners who lived before the incarnation of Christ, or (2) the rebellious angels of Genesis 6:1–4. *prison.* Likewise, the nature of this prison is not clear. It has been identified as: (1) hell, (2) a metaphor for the imprisonment that sin and ignorance brings, or (3) the world of spirits.

3:20 *eight people.* Noah and his wife and their three sons (Shem, Ham and Japheth) along with their wives.

3:21 *corresponds.* Peter is using metaphors to explain spiritual truth. *the pledge of a good conscience.* In baptism, we accept the privileges and responsibilities of following Christ. "Pledge" could also be translated "response." *saves you ... through the resurrection.* It is not the baptism in and of itself through which we find salvation. It is via Jesus that we are saved. It is to the resurrected Jesus that we pledge ourselves. It is the resurrection life of Jesus which we experience.

Living for God

SCRIPTURE 1 PETER 4:1–11

Last Week

Peter taught us the secret of how to love life in last week's session. We also considered how to prepare ourselves for the inevitable suffering that comes to those who follow Christ. This week we will consider again how important it is for Christians to be "clear-headed and disciplined" (4:7) in our approach to living lives of holiness.

Ice-Breaker   15 Min.

CONNECT WITH YOUR GROUP

LEADER

Begin the session with a word of prayer. Have your group members take turns sharing their responses to one, two or all three of the Ice-Breaker questions. Be sure that everyone gets a chance to participate.

New Year's Day is a popular time for people to make resolutions to improve their habits and behaviors. The trouble is January 2 comes way too fast. Many good intentions are often left in the dust due to lack of self-discipline. Take turns sharing your experiences with trying to change bad habits.

1. What were your New Year's resolutions for this year? How well have you kept them?

2. If you could add an hour to your day, how would you put it to use?

3. How much has your lifestyle changed in the past 10 years?

○ I am much more responsible.
○ I get involved in social issues.
○ I spend much less time sleeping.
○ My life is devoted to my family.
○ Other _____.

READ SCRIPTURE AND DISCUSS

Peter introduced a dichotomy, or duality, of our nature in chapter two—that we are both spirit and flesh. In this section he returns to that theme, urging us as followers of Christ to put to death the flesh and bring to life the spirit. This has many practical ramifications, including loving one another and avoiding the sins of the world around us. Read 1 Peter 4:1–11, and note how love is always our guide in living holy lives for God.

Living for God

4Therefore, since Christ suffered in the flesh, arm yourselves also with the same resolve—because the One who suffered in the flesh has finished with sin— 2in order to live the remaining time in the flesh, no longer for human desires, but for God's will. 3For there has already been enough time spent in doing the will of the pagans: carrying on in unrestrained behavior, evil desires, drunkenness, orgies, carousing, and lawless idolatry. 4In regard to this, they are surprised that you don't plunge with them into the same flood of dissipation—and they slander you. 5They will give an account to the One who stands ready to judge the living and the dead. 6For this reason the gospel was also preached to those who are now dead, so that, although they might be judged by men in the fleshly realm, they might live by God in the spiritual realm.

7Now the end of all things is near; therefore, be clear-headed and disciplined for prayer. 8Above all, keep your love for one another at full strength, since love covers a multitude of sins. 9Be hospitable to one another without complaining. 10Based on the gift they have received, everyone should use it to serve others, as good managers of the varied grace of God. 11If anyone speaks, his speech should be like the oracles of God; if anyone serves, his service should be from the strength God provides, so that in everything God may be glorified through Jesus Christ. To Him belong the glory and the power forever and ever. Amen.

1 Peter 4:1–11

QUESTIONS FOR INTERACTION

1. In what ways have your priorities changed as you've gotten older?

○ Not at all.
○ Completely.
○ Reordered but not replaced.
○ Replaced some, kept others.
○ Other _____.

2 What "resolve" does Peter tell us to arm ourselves with? How do we accomplish this?

3. How does "the will of the pagans" that Peter describes in verse 3 get carried out in our society today? What is to be our response?

4. How does one go about being "clear-headed and disciplined for prayer" (v. 7)?

5. Peter repeats the dichotomy of the "fleshly realm" and the "spiritual realm" that he introduced in 3:18. Why is it important for Christians to understand this concept? What effect can this attitude have on our lives?

6. Peter places love for one another as the highest priority—"above all" (v. 8). Why? How have you been doing at showing love to others lately?

7. In what ways can love cover a multitude of sins? How have some of your sins been covered by the love of another person?

GOING DEEPER:

If your group has time and/or wants a challenge, go on to this question.

8. What does Peter mean in verse 11, "If anyone speaks, his speech should be like the oracles of God?"

Caring Time 　　　　　　　　　　　　　　　　　　　　　15 Min.

APPLY THE LESSON AND PRAY FOR ONE ANOTHER

LEADER

Have you talked with your group about their mission—perhaps by sharing the vision of multiplying into two groups by the end of this study of 1 Peter? Is there someone in the group who could be a leader for a new small group when your group divides? How could you encourage and mentor that person?

Love covers a multitude of sins, and love for one another is the highest priority. Show this love to one another now through this time of sharing and prayer.

1 What changes is God calling you to make in your lifestyle? How can the group pray for you?

2 How strong is your resolve to do God's will at present?

3. How well is the group doing at keeping our love for one another at full strength?

Next Week

Today we considered the Lord's injunction to put to death the flesh and bring to life the spirit. This is accomplished both by abstaining from the wicked deeds of the world and by increasing our love for one another. In the coming week, spend time prayerfully searching your own life for areas of sin that may need to be put to death, and look for opportunities to serve someone in this group. Next week we will return to one of Peter's central themes in this letter, the fact that Christians often suffer.

Notes on 1 Peter 4:1–11

SUMMARY: The vindication that will be ours is coming, Peter says in this passage. Our sinful past is behind us. We do not have to face judgment on that account. And through Christ we will prevail over our tormentors (vv. 1–6). Furthermore, the end is near (v. 7). This being the case, we must strive to live out a lifestyle that is consistent with our calling (vv. 7–9), faithfully using the gifts of grace given us by God (vv. 10–11).

4:2 The "resolve" with which Christians are to "arm" themselves (v. 1) is stated here. That which determines the lifestyle of one who has been baptized into the death of Jesus is the will of God, not the desires of the flesh.

4:3 The list of vices here parallels the lists in Romans 13:13 and Galatians 5:19–21. The picture it paints is of a lifestyle characterized by sexual and alcoholic excess based on idolatry. This is a lifestyle out of control, arranged around harmful addictions and cultic practices. *time spent.* Christians have two views of time—time past, in which they gave themselves over to a destructive lifestyle, and "the remaining time in the flesh" (v. 2), that time following conversion in which they live in accord with God's will. *the will of the pagans.* The Christians to whom Peter writes are Gentiles rather than Jews, as this phrase shows. *unrestrained behavior.* "Excesses;" "outrages against decency;" "living in sensualities." *drunkenness.* Literally, "overflowings of wine." *carousing.* Literally, "drinking bouts;" "drunken parties."

4:4 Their pagan friends are astonished that they no longer lead this out-of-control lifestyle, but then their amazement turns into reaction and abuse. *slander.* There is plenty of evidence, from pagan as

well as Christian sources, that it was precisely the reluctance of Christians to participate in the routine of contemporary life, particularly conventionally accepted amusements, civic ceremonies, and any function involving contact with idolatry or what they considered immorality, that caused them to be hated, despised and themselves suspected of illicit practices.

4:5 This attitude will bring its own reward. These abusive pagans will themselves face judgment for their actions. *the living and the dead.* The final judgment will include both those who are still alive when Christ returns and those who have already died. All will face judgment.

4:6 *the gospel was also preached to those who are now dead.* The meaning of this phrase has been much debated. It probably refers to those members of the church who heard and accepted the Gospel but who have since died. Some scholars, however, connect this verse to 3:19–20 and conclude that this is a reference to Christ's descent into hell, during which he proclaimed the Gospel to those who were there. Some assert that those who heard Christ were those who lived prior to his coming and so never had a chance to hear the Gospel. Others feel that all the dead get the chance to hear the Gospel (and hence receive a second chance to come to faith). *judged by men in the fleshly realm.* This phrase may mean that death itself is a form of judgment. The body dies because it is sinful.

4:7–11 Peter gives yet another reason for forsaking their old, self-indulgent lifestyle: history is about to end. This is the time, he says, for self-discipline, prayer, and active love. In particular, they must care for each other. Mutuality is the key: mutual love (v. 8), mutual hospitality (v. 9), and mutual ministry (vv. 10–11).

4:7 *the end of all things.* The second coming of Jesus will mark the close of history when this world as it is now known passes away. *be clear-headed and disciplined.* As history draws to a close, our temptation might be to let their excitement get out of hand or to become self-indulgent. *for prayer.* When people are not thinking clearly or when their lives are out of control, they cannot pray properly.

4:8 Love is the key to a last-days' lifestyle. *love covers a multitude of sins.* A paraphrase of Proverbs 10:12. People tend to forgive those whom they love.

4:9 *Be hospitable.* This is one concrete way to show love. In a day when there were few decent hotels (most hotels were expensive, dirty, and bawdy), travelers depended on the willingness of others to take them in.

4:10 *gift.* This word is *charisma* and refers to the different gifts which the Holy Spirit gives to individual Christians for the sake of the whole body. *to serve others.* The point of these gifts is to use them for the sake of others. *the varied grace of God.* "Everyone" has a gift, but not all have the same gift. (See Rom. 12:6–8; 1 Cor. 12:7–10; Eph. 4:11–12 for lists of various gifts.)

4:11 Peter discusses two gifts in particular: the gift of teaching and preaching, and the gift of service. *If anyone speaks.* This is not the gift of tongues (ecstatic utterance, glossolalia) nor the gift of prophecy. The Greek word here refers to preaching and teaching. *if anyone serves.* There are different kinds of service: helping those in need, giving leadership, providing money (Acts 6:1–4; Rom. 12:13; 1 Cor. 12:5). *so that in everything God may be glorified.* The purpose of these gifts is to glorify God through their exercise, not to bring glory to the one with the gift.

Suffering for Christ

SCRIPTURE 1 PETER 4:12–19

Last Week

In our previous session, we learned that Christians need to be "clear-headed and disciplined" in their approach to holiness, and that love for one another is the highest priority. This week we will learn one of the reasons why these things are so important: suffering is a natural part of following Christ, simply because the one we follow had to suffer.

Ice-Breaker   15 Min.

CONNECT WITH YOUR GROUP

Getting sick is not fun, but to be sick and to be stuck with a long needle—well, that's the final humiliation. Take turns sharing how you are around doctors and needles, and other forms of suffering.

1. How did you react as a child when the doctor gave you a shot?

- ○ Stoic endurance.
- ○ Tasmanian devil.
- ○ Screaming meemie.
- ○ Passed out on the floor.
- ○ Other _____.

2. Have you ever had to go to court and stand before the judge? Tell us about it.

3. Who has been an encourager to you through a difficult time?

Bible Study

30 Min.

READ SCRIPTURE AND DISCUSS

Have one group member, whom you have selected beforehand, read aloud the Scripture passage. Then discuss the Questions for Interaction, dividing into subgroups of three to six.

Peter has not forgotten the suffering that his audience is facing, and in this passage he directly addresses the fact that they are undergoing real "fiery trials." But we are not to be surprised, he tells us, when Christians face trials, because the one we follow suffered terrible trials himself. Therefore, we as his disciples must expect to suffer as well. Read 1 Peter 4:12–19, and note how the secret to enduring suffering is to learn to trust our faithful Creator.

Suffering for Christ

12Dear friends, when the fiery ordeal arises among you to test you, don't be surprised by it, as if something unusual were happening to you. 13Instead, as you share in the sufferings of the Messiah rejoice, so that you may also rejoice with great joy at the revelation of His glory. 14If you are ridiculed for the name of Christ, you are blessed, because the Spirit of glory and of God rests on you. 15None of you, however, should suffer as a murderer, a thief, an evildoer, or as a meddler. 16But if anyone suffers as a Christian, he should not be ashamed, but should glorify God with that name. 17For the time has come for judgment to begin with God's household; and if it begins with us, what will the outcome be for those who disobey the gospel of God?

18And "if the righteous is saved with difficulty,
what will become of the ungodly and the sinner?"

19So those who suffer according to God's will should, in doing good, entrust themselves to a faithful Creator.

1 Peter 4:12–19

QUESTIONS FOR INTERACTION

Refer to the Summary and Study Notes at the end of this session as needed. If 30 minutes is not enough time to answer all of the questions in this section, conclude the Bible Study by answering questions 7 and 8.

1. When have you been in a situation where being a Christian wasn't very popular or accepted?

2. Note that Peter says in verse 12, "when the fiery ordeal arises among you." What does this suggest about the Christian life?

3. What are the purposes for which God sends "fiery trials" into a believer's life? What should our response be when they come? What should our response not be?

4. Why is it an honor to suffer for Christ?

5. What does it mean that "the Spirit of glory and of God rests on you" (v. 14) during times of trial? What are the implications of this?

6. Note the list of things in verse 15 for which Christians should not be suffering. Why does Peter list being a "meddler" on the same level with being a murderer? How is a meddler like a murderer or a thief?

7. How is rejoicing in suffering different from just enduring suffering? What effect has past suffering had on your commitment to God?

8. What is the ultimate secret for enduring trials (v. 19)? How does one do this? How are you doing at developing this attitude?

GOING DEEPER:

If your group has time and/or wants a challenge, go on to this question.

9. What does Peter mean when he says that judgment begins with God's household (v. 17)? What does "judgment" have to do with "fiery trials?"

Caring Time   15 Min.

APPLY THE LESSON AND PRAY FOR ONE ANOTHER

LEADER

Following the Caring Time, discuss with your group how they would like to celebrate the last session next week. Also, discuss the possibility of splitting into two groups or continuing together with another study.

Come together now and encourage one another to endure times of suffering and to trust our faithful Creator in all situations. Begin by sharing your responses to the following questions. Then share prayer requests and close in a group prayer.

1. Is anyone in the group undergoing a "fiery trial" at present? How can the group pray for you?

2. How well did you do at trusting your faithful Creator this past week? What could help you to trust him more in the future?

3. What can you do in the coming week to encourage someone who is going through a difficult time?

Next Week

Today we were confronted with the unpleasant fact that following Christ includes being prepared to suffer fiery trials. We took courage, however, from the fact that we have a Creator who is completely faithful, and we learned that the secret of preparing for trials is in developing the mindset of trusting in God. In the coming week, reach out to any in the group who are undergoing fiery trials. Next week will be our final study in 1 Peter, and we will return to the theme of submission. We will learn how developing important attitudes in our lives will carry us through trials and into God's glory.

Notes on 1 Peter 4:12–19

SUMMARY: Peter now moves into the final section of his letter in which he addresses the challenge facing these Asian Christians. He begins in this passage by focusing on the "fiery trial" they are going through. He does not introduce any new themes. Rather, he summarizes what he has already said in an intense and direct way as he encourages them to carry on in the face of their suffering. Suffering ought not to surprise them (v. 12), Peter says, nor should they be ashamed if they do suffer (v. 16). (He assumes that such suffering is because they bear the name of Christ, not because of wrongdoing.) Instead, they must rejoice (v. 13) and praise God (v. 16), knowing that they are participating in the sufferings of Christ (v. 13) and that the glory of God rests on them (v. 14). Furthermore, what they are going through is a sign that the end times have begun (v. 17). They know that these will culminate in the return of Christ at which point their suffering will end. They must remember that even though they are going through a hard time (v. 17) a far worse judgment will come upon their persecutors (vv. 17–18).

4:12–14 Both suffering and glory mark the life of the Christian. The glory is both in the future (v. 13) and in the present (v. 14).

4:12 *Dear friends.* With this form of address Peter begins the final section of his letter. The note of encouragement that he will sound in these remaining verses begins with this phrase. By it he reminds them once again that they are part of a loving fellowship. *fiery ordeal.* This word means "burning." It was used to describe cooking something over a fire or purifying a metal by fire. It is a vivid way to describe what was happening to them. This is the fourth time Peter has mentioned their trials (1:6–7; 2:19–23; 3:13–17). *don't be surprised.* In 4:4 he comments that their persecutors "are surprised" that they do not participate any longer in a debauched lifestyle. Here he uses the same verb but now it is their turn to be astonished. What they should not be surprised about is that they are persecuted.

4:13 *share.* In 2:20–21 Peter said that they were called to follow in Christ's steps. This they do when they suffer, even though they have only done what is good. In 4:1 he went a step further by reminding them that in their baptism they share in the death of Christ. Here he ties all this together by declaring that in this way they participate in the sufferings of Christ. *rejoice.* Rather than being bewildered ("surprised") at what is happening to them, they are actively to rejoice. They are not merely to passively endure these tri-

als. They must come to understand them as a way to participate in the experience of their Lord. This verb is in the present tense, signifying that what Peter is calling for is not a single response but an ongoing, continuous attitude of joy. This same attitude toward suffering is also found in Paul's epistle to the Philippians where joy is the central theme. *sufferings/glory.* The connection between suffering and glory is made at other points in the New Testament (Luke 6:22–23; Rom. 8:17; 2 Cor. 1:5–7; Phil. 3:10–11). *the revelation of His glory.* Peter has already reminded them that "the end of all things is near" (4:7). An awareness of this reality will enable them to cope with their suffering, not only because they know that their persecutors will one day have to answer to God for their deeds (4:5,17–18), but because at that point in time they will come into their share of the glory of Christ (see also 1:13). Once again, Peter looks forward to the day when Jesus returns and believers experience salvation fully.

4:14 *If you are ridiculed for the name of Christ, you are blessed.* The glory they experience is not only in the future. It is also in the here and now. *the Spirit of glory and of God rests on you.* Through the Holy Spirit they experience the glory of God (1:6,8). *glory.* In the Old Testament, the primary meaning of this word (*kabod*) is that of weight and substance. A man of wealth is a man of substance, of *kabod*. His external appearance and bearing would reflect his wealth, and also be called *kabod*. His wealth and dignity demanded and compelled respect and honor from his fellows, and this was called glory or honor. Hence weight, substance, wealth, dignity, noble bearing, and honor all contributed to its meaning. To these fundamental meanings Ezekiel added that of brightness. This word came to describe the actual, visible radiance of God himself. Glory is not just what God reflects; it is who he is. So in other words, these Asian Christians will (and do) share in the very nature of God himself.

4:15 Those that suffer because of wrongdoing do not gain this blessing. Peter's point (which he already made in 2:20) is that it is one thing to be punished for committing a crime (which was not why these Asian Christians were being persecuted), and quite another to be punished for doing good (which is what was happening to them). *murderer/thief/evildoer*. Each term connotes a recognizable form of wrongdoing which the civil authorities would clearly be justified in punishing (2:14). *meddler*. A busybody, someone who "sticks his nose" into other people's affairs. The Christian gains new insight into God's will, sees with newly opened spiritual eyes; but this spiritual sight is to be applied to oneself, not to one's neighbor. Peter warns his audience that they are not to be overly concerned with whether others are living according to the will of God.

4:16 *Christian*. Apart from two references in Acts 11:26 and Acts 26:28, this is the only use of "Christian" in the New Testament.

4:17 It is time for judgment to begin with the family of God. It was understood that in the last days the chosen people would suffer. This idea is found in the teaching of Jesus (Mark 13:8–13). In a sense, this is an encouraging sign. The tumultuous end times will precede the Second Coming, when it will be all over. When Christ returns, their inheritance and glory will begin. *what will the outcome be for those who disobey the gospel of God?* The judgment will also reach out to those who disobey God. By implication, this judgment will be far worse than the trials the Christians undergo (2 Thess. 1:5–10).

4:18 Peter confirms what he is saying by reference to Proverbs 11:31.

4:19 *entrust themselves*. This is a technical term which refers to the act of depositing money with a trusted friend. This is the same word Jesus used in Luke 23:46: "Father, into your hands I commit my spirit." In the end it all comes down to this. Those who suffer for doing good, those who suffer only because they are Christians (v. 16), must simply commit themselves to God. He is that trusted friend who can be relied upon absolutely to bear this trust. They will be safe with him.

SESSION 10
Be Humble and Sober
SCRIPTURE 1 PETER 5:1–14

 Last Week

Last week Peter focused on the fact that all Christians are called upon to face suffering and trials. In this section he returns to that topic, but only briefly. Clearly, his focus is not on the pain of suffering but on the glory that is to be revealed. With that in mind, he gives some parting exhortations on how to live our lives, whether facing persecution or peace. We are to live humbly and soberly resist the Devil, and above all we are to love one another.

Ice-Breaker   15 Min.

CONNECT WITH YOUR GROUP

LEADER

Begin this final session with a word of prayer and thanksgiving for this time together. Choose one or two Ice-Breaker questions to discuss.

Many of us are fortunate enough to have a mentor—someone who "takes us under his wing" and helps us along the journey of life. Peter was like that to his fellow Christians, and his words and teaching helped them through a very stressful time. Take turns sharing your thoughts and experiences with stress and mentors.

1. What do you do when you are anxious or stressed out?

○ Eat.
○ Stop eating.
○ Bite my nails.
○ Scream.
○ Withdraw.
○ Other _____.

2. Growing up, who was your best friend? What made him or her so special?

3. What teacher or leader do you have a great deal of respect for, and why?

READ SCRIPTURE AND DISCUSS

Peter closes his letter with some final advice. He returns to his theme of suffering, but it is interesting how he treats it. He is speaking to Christians who are facing torture and death at the hands of Nero, yet he refers to their suffering as though it were almost insignificant. This is not because he is callous, but rather because he is looking ahead, past the short-term suffering to the long-term glory that God will reveal very soon. With this attitude, says Peter, we can face trials with the understanding that they will not last long. In the meantime, we are to strive toward some important character qualities in our walk with God on earth. Read 1 Peter 5:1–14, and note the reasons we must be vigilant about our faith.

Be Humble and Sober

Reader One:
5 Therefore, as a fellow elder and witness to the sufferings of the Messiah, and also a participant in the glory about to be revealed, I exhort the elders among you: ²shepherd God's flock among you, not overseeing out of compulsion but freely, according to God's will; not for the money but eagerly; ³not lording it over those entrusted to you, but being examples to the flock. ⁴And when the chief Shepherd appears, you will receive the unfading crown of glory.

⁵Likewise, you younger men, be subject to the elders. And all of you clothe yourselves with humility toward one another, because

> "God resists the proud,
> but gives grace to the humble."

⁶Humble yourselves therefore under the mighty hand of God, so that He may exalt you in due time, ⁷casting all your care upon Him, because He cares about you.

Reader Two:
⁸Be sober! Be on the alert! Your adversary the Devil is prowling around like a roaring lion, looking for anyone he can devour. ⁹Resist him, firm in the faith, knowing that the same sufferings are being experienced by your brothers in the world.

¹⁰Now the God of all grace, who called you to His eternal glory in Christ Jesus, will personally restore, establish, strengthen, and support you after you have suffered a little. ¹¹To Him be the dominion forever. Amen.

¹²Through Silvanus, whom I consider a faithful brother, I have written briefly, encouraging you and testifying that this is the true grace of God. Take your stand in it! ¹³She who is in Babylon, also chosen, sends you greetings, as does Mark, my son. ¹⁴Greet one another with a kiss of love. Peace to all of you who are in Christ.

1 Peter 5:1–14

QUESTIONS FOR INTERACTION

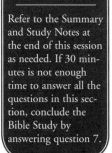

Refer to the Summary and Study Notes at the end of this session as needed. If 30 minutes is not enough time to answer all the questions in this section, conclude the Bible Study by answering question 7.

1. According to Peter, what are some of the qualities of the elder or shepherd of a congregation? How should an elder teach his flock? Which of these qualities do you appreciate in your church's pastor or elders?

2. What does it mean to "clothe yourselves with humility?" What (or who) are some practical examples of this?

3. What is to be the attitude of those who are under the care of an elder?

4. What does it mean in practical terms to be "sober" and "on the alert" (v. 8)?

   ○ To study the Word of God and seek to understand it with other Christians.
   ○ To stay away from tempting situations.
   ○ To stay away from non-Christians.
   ○ To take time every day to pray and listen to God.
   ○ Other _____.

5. How does one resist the Devil? What happens when we do? What happens when we don't?

6. Peter states that God "will personally restore, establish, strengthen, and support you after you have suffered a little" (v. 10). Have you experienced this in your life? In what way?

7. In our study of 1 Peter, what has been the key thing you have learned? How are you doing at putting that lesson into practice?

GOING DEEPER:

If your group has time and/or wants a challenge, go on to this question.

8. What does it mean that "God resists the proud, but gives grace to the humble" (v. 5)? How and why does he resist the proud? What "grace" does he give to the humble?

Caring Time   15 Min.

APPLY THE LESSON AND PRAY FOR ONE ANOTHER

LEADER

Conclude this final Caring Time by praying for each group member and asking for God's blessing in any plans to start a new group or continue to study together.

Gather around each other now in this final time of sharing and prayer and encourage one another to have faith and hope as you go back out into the world.

1. Do you need help resisting the Devil right now? How can the group or someone in it assist you?

2. Is there someone in this group who has particularly taught you by example?

3. What has the group decided to do next? What is the next step for you personally?

Notes on 1 Peter 5:1–14

SUMMARY: Peter ends his letter by addressing the question of how the church ought to function during a time of suffering (vv. 1–11). First, he examines the responsibilities of the elders (vv. 1–4). Second, he looks briefly at the responsibilities of younger church members (v. 5). Then, third, he comments on the responsibilities of all church members (vv. 6–7). Finally, he concludes by reminding them that they are, in fact, engaged in spiritual warfare (vv. 8–11). Satan is behind all their troubles. He ends his letter in typical fashion with personal greetings and a benediction (vv. 12–14).

5:1 *elders.* The leaders of the local congregation who probably functioned in the same way as the board of elders in a synagogue, having administrative and spiritual responsibility for the congregation. *a fellow elder.* Peter bears the same sort of responsibility they do. Thus he understands the pressures and the problems they face. *witness.* The Greek word is *martus,* from which "martyr" is derived. Strictly speaking, what Peter is saying is that he was an eyewitness of the death of Jesus. He is therefore able to point to Jesus in his suffering as an example they are to follow (2:21). In the New Testament, this word came to mean one who bears witness to Jesus (Luke 24:48; Acts 1:8; 22:15). Eventually it was applied to those who suffered because of their witness (Acts 22:20; Rev. 2:13; 11:3, 7). Thus it came into English as "martyr."

5:2 *shepherd.* This is a command. They cannot be passive or slack in what they do. They need to attend to their job of caring for God's people. *God's flock.* The idea that the people of God are like a flock of sheep and that their leaders are like shepherds is found in a number of places in the Old Testament (Ps. 23; Isa. 40:11; Jer. 23:1–4; Ezek. 34). *overseeing.* This was the main job of an elder: supervising the affairs of the community. This phrase later came to mean "function as a bishop." Peter follows this general admonition with three phrases, each expressed in an antithetical way, by which he defines the spirit in which they are to hold this office. *not overseeing out of compulsion but freely.* The first of three antitheses. Here the contrast is between reluctant and willing service. The elders should be willing volunteers in God's service. *not for the money but eagerly.* The second antithesis: between service in order to profit financially and service based on zeal for God. In all likelihood, elders received some financial remuneration (1 Cor. 9:7–12; 1 Tim. 5:17–18).

The temptation might be to regard their office simply as a job and not as a calling.

5:3 *not lording it over those entrusted to you, but being examples.* The third antithesis: between domineering over those you are to care for and coming to them in humility. Peter has already defined how the community ought to function (2:13–3:12). Mutual respect, submission, humility, and love are the attitudes which should characterize the Christian community, and the elders would be expected to set an example in displaying these attitudes. *those entrusted to you.* This phrase probably refers to splitting up the flock into groups, each of which would be under the care of a particular elder.

5:4 *chief Shepherd.* Peter has already described Jesus as the "Shepherd" (2:25). Here he adds an adjective that reminds the elders that their authority is not absolute, but derived from Jesus. *crown of glory.* The victor at an athletic event in a Greek city had a garland of ivy or bay placed on his head. Citizens who performed outstanding service to the city were also given such crowns. The image of the crown became a common New Testament symbol for the reward promised to Christians (1 Cor. 9:25; 2 Tim. 4:8; James 1:12; Rev. 2:10). Peter says that this crown will consist of the "glory" of Christ which will be revealed at the Second Coming.

5:5 *Likewise.* Probably a reference to 2:13–3:12, where Peter considered the question of how to relate to those who are above you in the social order. In that earlier section, the question was how to relate to those in secular society who have the potential to oppress you (rulers, slave owners, pagan husbands). Here the issue is how to relate to those in the church who are leaders. *younger men.* The Greek social order was such that young men were considered subordinate to older men. *be subject.* Submission and respect are called for once again. *clothe yourselves with humility.* This is a rare verb, meaning "wrap yourselves" or "gird yourselves." It is derived from the name for the apron which was worn by slaves when working. It conjures up an image of Jesus who wrapped a towel around himself when he washed the feet of the disciples (John 13:4), an act which is the perfect demonstration of what humility is all about. There is an untranslated word which begins this sentence (*pantes* or "all") which marks a shift in focus from a brief admonition to younger men to instructions for all Christians.

5:6 *Humble yourselves.* The same humility which is owed one another is owed God as well. *that He may exalt you in due time.* This will happen when Christ returns and they experience his glory.

5:7 *casting all your care upon Him.* This verb should be translated as a participle ("casting"), not as an imperative ("cast"), since in Greek it is connected to the imperative "humble yourself." It is not a separate commandment.

5:8 *Be sober! Be on the alert!* They are not to be passive in the face of trouble. Coupled with conscious reliance on God, there must also be diligent effort on their part. *the Devil.* Behind all their trials stands the devil (*diabolos*). In the Old Testament he is known by the Hebrew name Satan. In the New Testament he is seen as the one who tempts (as he did with Jesus), as the Prince of Evil who rebelled against God, as the Antichrist, and as the one who seeks to undo God's purposes.

5:9 *Resist him.* Peter's advice is plain: do not run away, stand your ground and face him, refuse to give in to his purposes, trust in God (Eph. 6:10–13; Jam. 4:7; Rev. 12:9–11). *the same sufferings are being experienced by your brothers in the world.* Solidarity with Christian brothers and sisters around the world is a strong motivation for standing firm.

5:10–11 Satan may be their enemy and he is powerful and vicious ("like a roaring lion looking for someone to devour"), but he is no match for God. Assurance of strength and victory is another motivation for continuing to resist evil.

5:12–14 Peter concludes his letter, as do most letters in the New Testament, with greetings and personal comments.

5:12 *Silvanus.* Like Paul and others, Peter used an amanuensis (secretary or scribe) to write this letter.

In this case, Silvanus seems to have had an active part in shaping the final form of the letter with its rather polished Greek. The Silvanus referred to here is probably the Silas (a variant of the same name) who was Paul's companion on his second missionary trip (Acts 15:40–18:5), a minister of the Gospel (2 Cor. 1:19), and the coauthor with Paul of 1 and 2 Thessalonians.

5:13 *She who is in Babylon ... sends you greetings.* Peter is probably referring to the church (2 John 1,13) in Rome, where he was when he wrote this letter. ***Mark, my son.*** Tradition has it that Mark was another of Peter's secretaries; and, in writing the Gospel that bears his name, Mark was expressing Peter's experience of Jesus. Certainly this phrase reflects a warm relationship between the two.

5:14 *a kiss of love.* At some point during the worship service, Christians would greet each other with an embrace, signifying their close bonds as brothers and sisters in the Lord. This was a ritual developed by the church and not, as in so many other cases, adopted from Jewish liturgy.